**LEVEL D**

STECK-VAUGHN

# FOCUS ON SCIENCE

**PROGRAM CONSULTANT**
Elizabeth Maryott
Instructor, Mathematics-Science Division
Wayne State College
Wayne, Nebraska

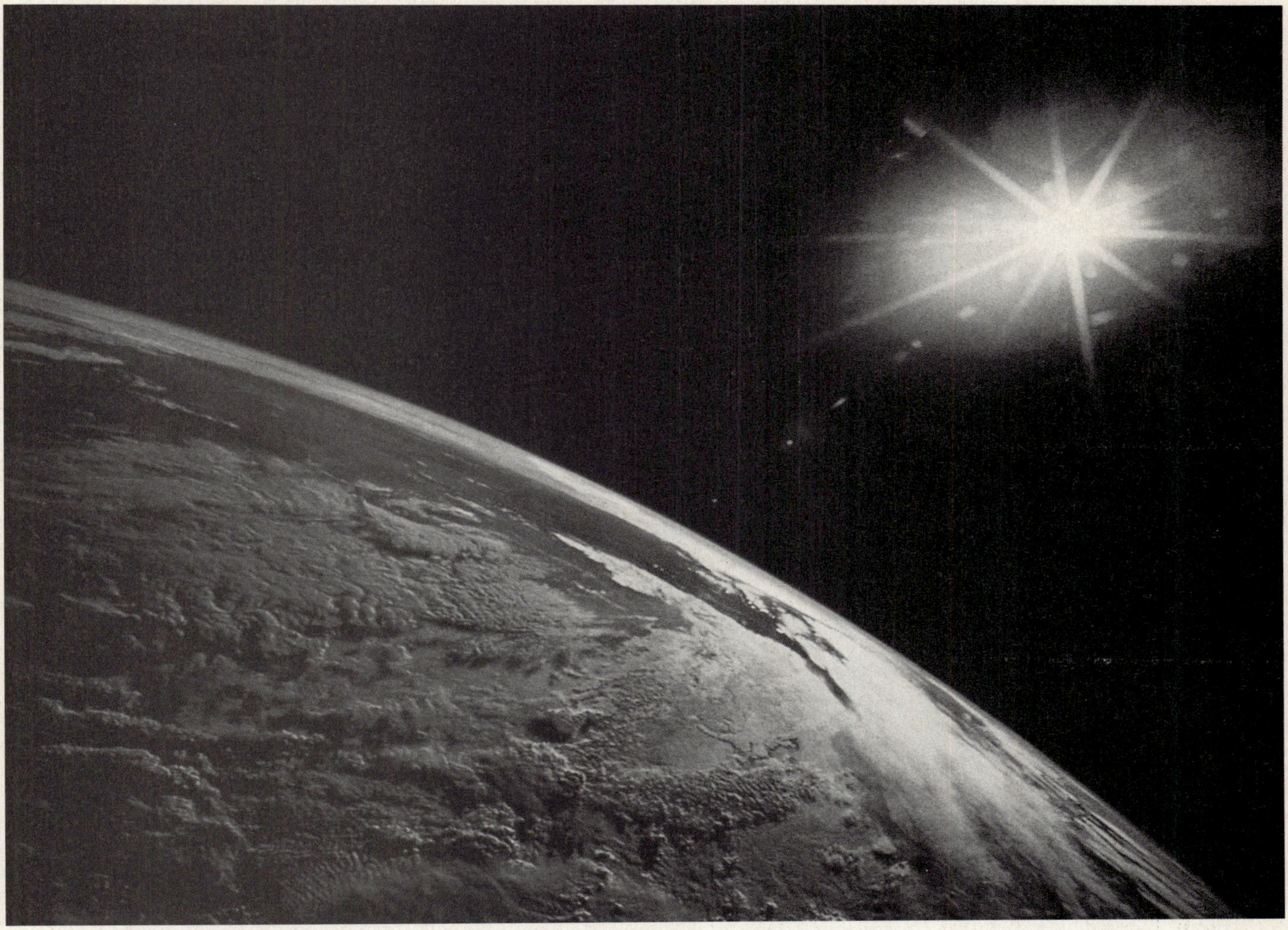

STECK-VAUGHN
COMPANY

*A Division of Harcourt Brace & Company*

# Acknowledgments

## STAFF CREDITS

**Executive Editor:** Diane Sharpe
**Project Team Leaders:** Jim Cauthron, Design; Janet Jerzycki, Editorial
**Editor:** Linda Bullock
**Design Manager:** Jim Cauthron
**Cover Design:** Jim Cauthron
**Cover Electronic Production:** Alan Klemp
**Program Development, Design, Illustration, and Production:**
Proof Positive/Farrowlyne Associates, Inc.

## PHOTOGRAPHY AND ILLUSTRATION CREDITS

Cover and Title page © PhotoDisk; p. 5 Tim Flach/Tony Stone Images; p. 6 © PhotoDisk; p. 7 © PhotoDisk; p. 8 Leslie Dunlap; p. 9 Tek-Nēk, Inc.; p. 10a Corel Photo Studio; p. 10b Michael Eichelberger/Visuals Unlimited; p. 12 Tek-Nēk, Inc.; p. 14 Tek-Nēk, Inc.; p. 16 David L Pearson/Visuals Unlimited; p. 18a John Gerlach/Visuals Unlimited; p. 18b Tek-Nēk, Inc.; p. 20 Kathie Kelleher; p. 22 Art Wolfe/Tony Stone Images; p. 23 © PhotoDisk; p. 24 Sandy McMahon; p. 27 Sandy McMahon; p. 28 Sandy McMahon; p. 30 Leslie Dunlap; p. 32 Joel Snyder; p. 34 Corel Photo Studio; p. 36 Kathie Kelleher; p. 38 William J. Weber/Visuals Unlimited; p. 39 © PhotoDisk; p. 40 Sandy McMahon; p. 42 Tek-Nēk, Inc.; p. 44 Tek-Nēk, Inc.; p. 46 Tek-Nēk, Inc.; p. 48 Tek-Nēk, Inc.; p. 49 Tek-Nēk, Inc.; p. 50 David Griffen; p. 52 Kathie Kelleher; p. 54a Randy Urie/Stock Market; p. 54b Kjell B Sandved/Visuals Unlimited; p. 54c Jose Pelaez/The Stock Market; p. 55 Paul Chesley/Tony Stone Images; p. 56 Jane McAlonan/Visuals Unlimited; p. 57 © PhotoDisk; p. 58 Kathie Kelleher; p. 59 Tek-Nēk, Inc.; p. 60 Tek-Nēk, Inc.; p. 61 Tek-Nēk, Inc.; p. 62 Kathie Kelleher; p. 63 Kathie Kelleher; p. 64 Joel Snyder; p. 66a Alan Oddie/PhotoEdit; p. 66b Daniel Gotshall/Visuals Unlimited; p. 68 Joel Snyder; p. 70 Kathie Kelleher; p. 72 Terry Donnelly/Tony Stone Images; p. 73 © PhotoDisk; p. 74 Leslie Dunlap; p. 76a Corel Photo Studio; p. 76b Les Christman/Visuals Unlimited; p. 76c Corel Photo Studio; p. 78 Tek-Nēk, Inc.; p. 80 Leslie Dunlap; p. 82a Leslie Dunlap; p. 84 Corel Photo Studio; p. 86 Joel Snyder; p. 88 Bill & Sally Fletcher/Tom Stack & Associates; p. 89 © PhotoDisk; p. 90a Tek-Nēk, Inc.; p. 90b NASA/Newell Colour Imaging; p. 92 Tek-Nēk, Inc.; p. 94a Tek-Nēk, Inc.; p. 94b Corel Photo Studio; p. 96 NASA/NASA Media Services; p. 96d Corel Photo Studio; p. 98a Corel Photo Studio; p. 98b Corel Photo Studio; p. 98c NASA/NASA Media Services; p. 98d NASA/NASA Media Services; p. 98e NASA/NASA Media Services; p. 100 Tek-Nēk, Inc.; p. 102 Joel Snyder; p. 104a Rick Poley/Visuals Unlimited; p. 104b Corel Photo Studio; p. 104c Tony Freeman/PhotoEdit; p. 105 Scott Liles/Unicorn Stock Photos; p. 106 Barbara Filet/Tony Stone Images; p. 107 © PhotoDisk; p. 108 Tek-Nēk, Inc.; p. 110 Chris Windle; p. 112 Tek-Nēk, Inc.; p. 114 Chris Windle; p. 116 Joel Snyder; p. 118 Chris Windle; p. 119 Chris Windle; p. 120 Joel Snyder; p. 122a Corel Photo Studio; p. 122b Firefly Productions/The Stock Market; p. 122c Diane Hirsch/Fundamental Photographs

ISBN: 0-8172-8030-8

Copyright © 1999 Steck-Vaughn Company
All rights reserved. No part of the material protected by this copyright may be reproduced in any form by any means, electronic or mechanical, including photocopying, recording, or by any information storage and retrieval system, without permission in writing from the copyright owner. Requests for permission to make copies of any part of the work should be mailed to: Copyright Permissions, Steck-Vaughn Company, P.O. Box 26015, Austin, Texas 78755. Printed in the United States of America.
1 2 3 4 5 6 7 8 9 0 DBH 04 03 02 01 00 99 98

# Contents

## Unit 1 ■ Life Science ... 5

### Chapter 1 How Plants Live and Grow ... 6
- **Lesson 1** What Are the Parts of Plants? ... 8
- **Lesson 2** What Are Cells? ... 10
- **Lesson 3** How Do Plants Get Energy? ... 12
- **Lesson 4** How Do Materials Move Through Plants? ... 14
- **Lesson 5** How Do Plants Grow and Change? ... 16
- **Lesson 6** How Do Plants Reproduce? ... 18
- Chapter 1 Hands-On Activity ... 20
- Chapter 1 Test ... 21

### Chapter 2 How Animals Live and Grow ... 22
- **Lesson 1** What Are Animals? ... 24
- **Lesson 2** How Are Animals Grouped? ... 26
- **Lesson 3** How Do Animals Use Oxygen, Water, and Food? ... 28
- **Lesson 4** How Do Animals Change? ... 30
- **Lesson 5** How Do People Grow and Change? ... 32
- **Lesson 6** What Are Characteristics? ... 34
- Chapter 2 Hands-On Activity ... 36
- Chapter 2 Test ... 37

### Chapter 3 Your Senses ... 38
- **Lesson 1** How Can You Learn About the World? ... 40
- **Lesson 2** How Do the Eyes Work? ... 42
- **Lesson 3** How Do the Ears Work? ... 44
- **Lesson 4** How Do Taste and Smell Work? ... 46
- **Lesson 5** What Is Touch? ... 48
- **Lesson 6** How Can You Protect Your Senses? ... 50
- Chapter 3 Hands-On Activity ... 52
- Chapter 3 Test ... 53

**Unit 1 Careers** ... 54

## Unit 2 ■ Earth Science ... 55

### Chapter 4 The Living Earth ... 56
- **Lesson 1** What Is an Ecosystem? ... 58
- **Lesson 2** What Lives in an Ecosystem? ... 60
- **Lesson 3** How Do Living Things Compete? ... 62
- **Lesson 4** How Do Ecosystems Change? ... 64
- **Lesson 5** How Do People Change Ecosystems? ... 66
- **Lesson 6** How Can People Protect Ecosystems? ... 68
- Chapter 4 Hands-On Activity ... 70
- Chapter 4 Test ... 71

## Chapter 5 Earth's Surface ............................................. 72
### Lesson 1 What Are Landforms? ......................... 74
### Lesson 2 How Do Landforms Change Slowly? ...... 76
### Lesson 3 How Do Landforms Change Quickly? ..... 78
### Lesson 4 How Do Rocks Form and Change? ........ 80
### Lesson 5 What Is the Ocean Like? ..................... 82
### Lesson 6 How Do People Affect the Ocean? ........ 84
### Chapter 5 Hands-On Activity ........................... 86
### Chapter 5 Test ................................................ 87

## Chapter 6 Our Solar System ............................................ 88
### Lesson 1 What Tools Do Astronomers Use? ........ 90
### Lesson 2 What Is Our Solar System? .................. 92
### Lesson 3 What Is the Moon? ............................ 94
### Lesson 4 What Are the Inner Planets? ................ 96
### Lesson 5 What Are the Outer Planets? ............... 98
### Lesson 6 What Are Comets, Asteroids, and Meteoroids? ........ 100
### Chapter 6 Hands-On Activity ........................... 102
### Chapter 6 Test ................................................ 103

## Unit 2 Careers ............................................................... 104

# Unit 3 ■ Physical Science .................................................. 105

## Chapter 7 Energy ........................................................... 106
### Lesson 1 What Is Light? .................................... 108
### Lesson 2 How Does Light Travel? ...................... 110
### Lesson 3 What Is Sound? .................................. 112
### Lesson 4 What Is a Magnet? ............................. 114
### Lesson 5 How Is Electricity Used? ...................... 116
### Lesson 6 What Is a Circuit? ............................... 118
### Chapter 7 Hands-On Activity ........................... 120
### Chapter 7 Test ................................................ 121

## Unit 3 Careers ............................................................... 122
### Glossary ....................................................... 123

# Unit 1
# Life Science

All living things need food to live and grow. The plant in the picture makes its own food using sunlight. The hummingbird cannot make its own food. Just like you, it must eat food. In this unit you will learn how plants and animals live and grow. You will also learn how your senses, such as sight and hearing, tell you about your world.

CHAPTER 1

# How Plants Live and Grow

Imagine you are standing in the woods. It is peaceful and quiet. You look at a green leaf. The leaf is completely still. You can't tell, but this leaf is busy! It is taking in water and air, making food, and growing. How does it do it? In this chapter you will learn all about plants.

What is it?

- It is too small to see with just your eyes.
- It is the smallest part of all living things.
- In plants, different ones do different jobs.

# LESSON 1
## What Are the Parts of Plants?

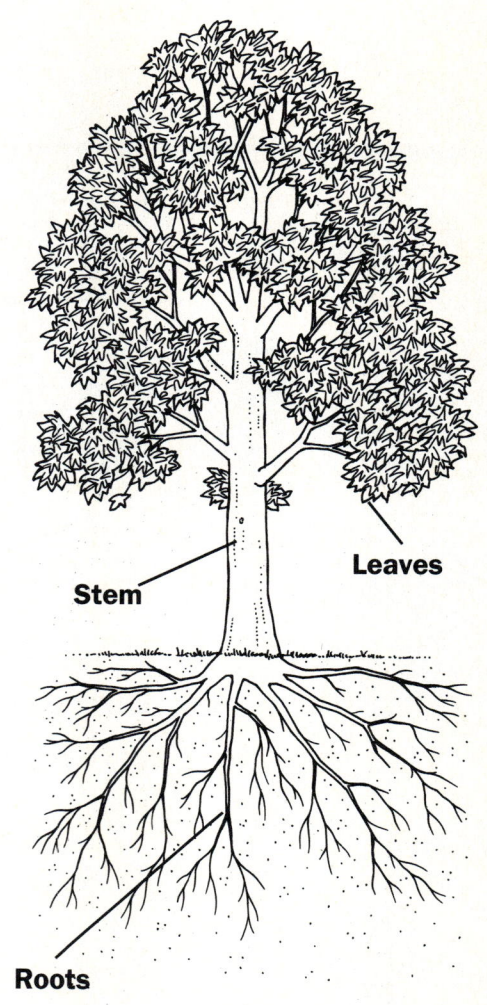

**Parts of a Tree**

There are many different kinds of plants. Giant oaks, tiny roses, and banana trees are all plants. Even though different kinds of plants are different from one another, they are alike in some ways. Most plants have three main parts—**roots**, **stems**, and **leaves**. Each of these parts helps plants live and grow.

**Roots** take up water and other materials that plants need from the soil. Roots also hold plants in the soil. Different kinds of roots grow in different kinds of soil. Some plants that grow in sand have many thin roots spread out over a wide area. These roots can take in water quickly. Other plants have thick roots that grow deep into the soil.

**Stems** help hold plants up. They also help carry water and food through plants. Stems can be tall or short. They can be thick or thin. Trees have tall, thick stems called trunks, but beans have shorter, thinner stems.

Most of a plant's food is made in its **leaves**. Like stems and roots, leaves come in many sizes and shapes. They may be long and wide, like the leaves on a palm tree. Or they may be short and sharp, like the needles on a pine tree. Although leaves can be different colors such as red or purple, they are usually green. They may be smooth or rough. Their edges may be round or pointed. Most leaves only live a short time on plants. Then, they fall and new leaves appear to take their place.

**A.** Write the missing word in each sentence.

1. The three main parts of plants are roots, stems, and _____.
   (trunks, food, leaves)

2. Roots take in water from the _____.
   (stem, soil, leaves)

3. Trunks are the thick _____ of trees.
   (stems, leaves, roots)

4. Leaves are the part of the plant where _____ is made.
   (water, soil, food)

**B.** Label the picture with the correct name for each plant part.

Roots

Leaves

Stem

**C.** Write one or more sentences to answer the question.

Large trees usually have many roots that grow into the ground. How might these roots help the tree in windy weather?

_____

_____

9

## LESSON 2
# What Are Cells?

You already know a lot about plants and their parts. You can show someone a leaf, a stem, or a root. But do you know that these parts of plants are made of smaller parts called **cells**? The cell is the smallest part of all living things.

Most cells are too small to see without a **microscope**. A microscope is a tool that makes objects look larger. If you put a piece of a leaf under a microscope, you would see leaf cells. Plant cells look like rows of bricks. All plant cells are not alike. Different parts of plants have different kinds of cells. A root cell is different from a leaf cell.

Thinking about bricks, walls, buildings, and towns can help you understand something about plants. Groups of bricks may be parts of walls. Walls may be parts of buildings. Buildings may be parts of towns.

Cells are like bricks. Groups of cells working together are called **tissues**. Tissues are like the walls. Tissues make leaves, stems, and roots, which are like the buildings. Plants are like the towns. In all living things, smaller parts make up larger parts. That is why we say that living things show **organization**. Parts work together to help living things grow.

Of course, cells are different from bricks. Each cell in a plant has a job to do. For example, root cells take in water that the plant needs. Leaf cells use the water when they make food for the plant. Root and leaf cells work together so the plant can live and grow.

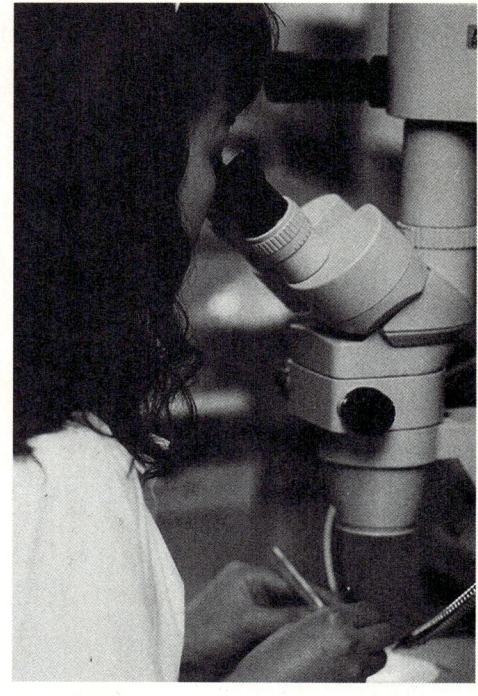
People use microscopes to see cells.

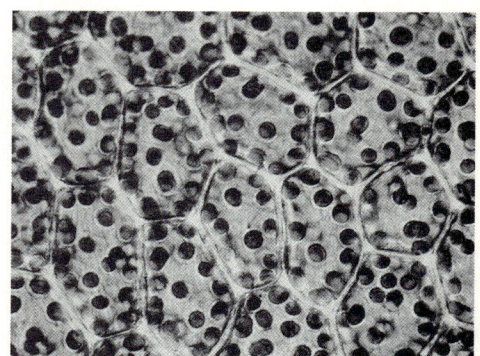
This picture shows what leaf cells look like under a microscope.

**A.** Write the missing word in each sentence.

1. All living things are made of _____.
   (cells, roots, organization)

2. Most cells are too small to see unless you use a _____.
   (stem, microscope, tissue)

3. Leaves, stems, and roots are made of _____.
   (organization, tissues, bricks)

**B.** Write **True** if the sentence is true. Write **False** if the sentence is false.

_____ 1. Each cell in a plant has a job to do.

_____ 2. Root cells and leaf cells are the same.

_____ 3. All of the cells in a plant work together so that the plant can stay alive.

**C.** All living things show organization. Write the words in the correct box.

cells    leaves    plants    tissues

[_____] are parts of [_____] are parts of

[_____] are parts of [_____]

**D.** Write one or more sentences to answer the questions.

How are cells like bricks? How are they different from bricks?

_____
_____
_____
_____

11

# LESSON 3: How Do Plants Get Energy?

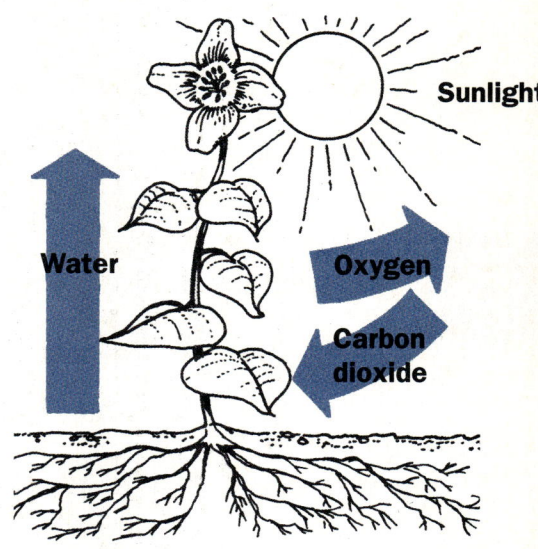

**Photosynthesis**

All living things use energy from food to live and grow. You know that plant cells make their own food. Several steps happen when plant cells make food. The group of steps is called a **process**.

The process that plants use to make food is called **photosynthesis**. Plants need three things to make food. They need light, a gas called **carbon dioxide**, and water. Light comes from the sun. Carbon dioxide comes from the air. Water comes from the soil.

Light is a kind of energy. In photosynthesis, plants use light energy and change it to food energy. How do plants get light energy? Leaves make a chemical called **chlorophyll**. The chlorophyll in leaves traps light from the sun. Even on cloudy days, chlorophyll traps some light from the sun.

Carbon dioxide is part of the air all around Earth. You can't see carbon dioxide. It enters plants through small openings in the leaves called **stomata**. With light from the sun, plants use carbon dioxide and water to make a special kind of sugar. The sugar is the food that plants need to live and grow.

While plants make food, they give off some **oxygen**. Like carbon dioxide, oxygen is a gas. It moves from the stomata out into the air we breathe. Animals, including humans, could not live without oxygen from plants.

## A. Write the word or words that best complete each sentence.

carbon dioxide     food     photosynthesis
chlorophyll     oxygen     plants

1. All living things get energy from _____.

2. A green chemical called _____ traps light from the sun.

3. The process plants use to make food is called _____.

4. Plants need water, _____, and light to make their own food.

5. Plants give off a gas called _____.

6. Animals could not live without oxygen from _____.

## B. Draw a line to complete each sentence.

1. Roots     traps light from the sun.
2. Stomata     moves from the plant into the air.
3. Chlorophyll     let carbon dioxide enter the plant.
4. Oxygen     take in water from the ground.

## C. Write one or more sentences to answer the question.

Why is light important to plants?

_____

_____

_____

# LESSON 4: How Do Materials Move Through Plants?

Materials move around in plants through tubes called **xylem** and **phloem**. Water, food, and **nutrients** move through the xylem and phloem. Nutrients are special matter that plants need to grow and stay healthy. These nutrients are in the soil. They enter a plant through the roots.

**Xylem** moves water and nutrients from the roots to the stems and leaves. **Phloem** moves food around the plant. The roots, stems, and leaves need food to live and grow.

When a plant makes more food than it needs right away, it stores the food. Phloem carries food to be stored in stems or roots. Later on, the plant may need this stored food in its leaves. The food can travel again through the phloem, back up the stems, and out to the leaves.

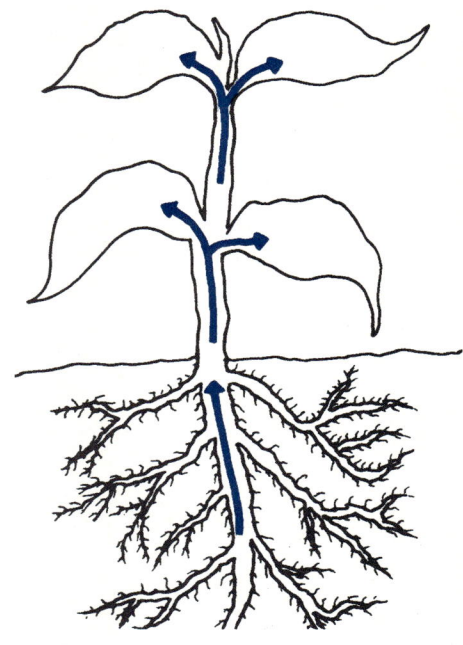

Water moves through xylem from roots up to leaves.

Humans and other animals use food energy stored in plants. You eat different parts of many plants. The orange part of a carrot is its root. When you eat a carrot, you are eating the food that the phloem carried to the root. In other plants, phloem carries food to the stems. Celery and sugarcane are two plants that store food in their stems. And when you eat lettuce, you are eating the food the plant stored in its leaves.

If you have ever looked inside the trunk of a tree that has been cut, you may see rings. These rings are xylem. You can count the rings of xylem to learn how old the tree is. The rings can also tell you something about the place where the tree lived. If the rings are wide, the tree had lots of light, water, and nutrients to grow.

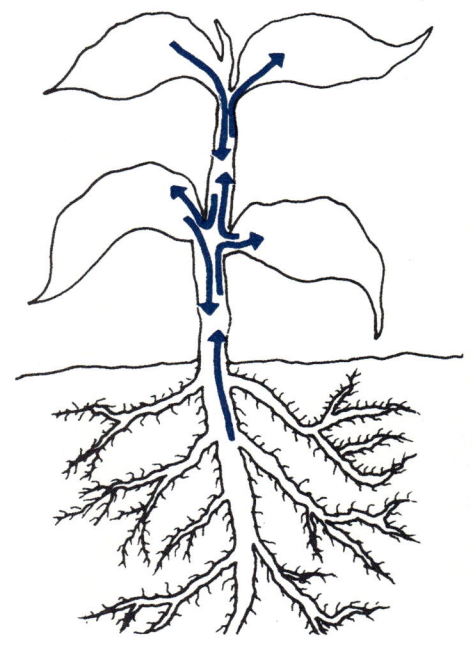

Food moves through phloem to and from leaves and roots.

**A.** Write <u>xylem</u>, <u>phloem</u>, or <u>both</u> to answer each question.

1. Which carries water through a plant? _____
2. Which moves food through a plant? _____
3. Which are tubes that move materials through plants?
   _____
4. Which carries food to be stored in stems?
   _____

**B.** Draw a picture of a plant. Use arrows to show how food, water, and materials move through xylem and phloem.

[ ]

**C.** Write one or more sentences to answer the questions.

In spring, some people collect a sweet liquid from maple trees. This liquid is cooked until it becomes maple syrup. Do you think the sweet liquid comes from the xylem or the phloem of the tree? Why?

_____
_____
_____

# LESSON 5

# How Do Plants Grow and Change?

All living things make changes when something in their surroundings changes. For example, if it gets dark, you might turn on a light. A plant can't turn on a light. But plants also make changes that help them live and grow.

Plants make changes to light in a few ways. You know that plants need light to make food. Most stems and leaves grow up toward the sun. By growing toward the sun, leaves get the light they need to carry out photosynthesis. You also know that plants need water and nutrients from the soil. So, roots grow down into the soil toward the center of Earth.

Some trees keep their leaves all year.

Many plants live in places where the seasons change. In winter, for example, temperatures are cool and water may freeze. The sun doesn't shine for much of the day. When these changes happen, plants change, too. Many plants lose their leaves before winter comes. They do not grow as much during the fall and winter. Then, they grow new leaves when the spring comes again.

Some plants live in places that are very dry. In deserts, rain may fall for only a short time each year. Desert plants make changes to save water. During the hot, sunny days, the flowers on some desert plants close. Then, they open again during the cool nights.

Plants make changes in other ways. Some plants change when they are touched. If you touch one of these plants, the leaves may fold up. Also, the branches of the plant may fall down against the stem of the plant.

Some trees lose their leaves in the fall and grow new ones in the spring.

**A.** Write <u>True</u> if the sentence is true. Write <u>False</u> if the sentence is false.

_____ 1. Plants are the only living things that make changes when change happens in their surroundings.

_____ 2. All trees lose their leaves before winter arrives.

_____ 3. Some trees grow more slowly during winter.

_____ 4. Some plants change by folding up their leaves when they are touched.

**B.** Write the missing word or words in each sentence.

1. Leaves grow toward _____.
   (darkness, light, the center of Earth)

2. Plant roots grow toward _____.
   (darkness, light, the center of Earth)

3. Plants that live in deserts make changes to save
   _____.
   (water, light, soil)

**C.** Put a ✔ next to the ways that plants make changes.

_____ 1. Flowers on plants in deserts close during the day.

_____ 2. Plants do not change.

_____ 3. Some trees lose their leaves in the fall.

_____ 4. All roots grow toward light.

**D.** Write one or more sentences to answer the question.

How does growing new leaves help plants?

_____

_____

_____

## LESSON 6

# How Do Plants Reproduce?

Growing and changing are parts of life. The way a living thing grows and changes is called its **life cycle**. Birth, growth, adulthood, and death are parts of the life cycle.

During every complete life cycle, there is a time when a living thing can **reproduce**. When a plant reproduces, it makes new plants like itself. Many plants reproduce through seeds. In a complete life cycle, seeds grow into adult plants that can make new seeds.

Where do seeds come from? Some plants have flowers. These plants are called **flowering plants**. Seeds form inside flowers. Flowers have both male and female parts. The male part makes tiny grains called **pollen**. The female part makes **eggs**. Eggs and pollen come together to form a seed.

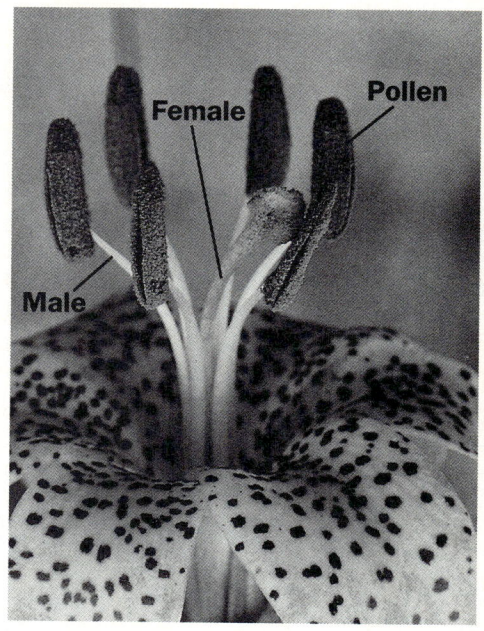

Seeds form inside flowers on flowering plants.

Not all plants have flowers. Some plants make seed cones. These plants are called **conifers**. Conifers make both male and female cones. The male cones make pollen. The female cones make eggs. Pollen from male cones joins with eggs in female cones to make seeds.

Some seeds grow into new plants. To grow into a new plant, a seed needs soil, space, and water. Some seeds, such as dandelion seeds, are light. The wind carries light seeds to places where they might grow. Some seeds are sticky. These seeds can stick to the fur of animals. As the animals move, the seeds move with them. The seeds may fall off the animals and grow in a new place.

Conifers make seeds in cones.

## A. Write the missing word or words in each sentence.

1. All living things have _____.
   (seeds, flowers, a life cycle)

2. Once plants become _____, they are able to reproduce.
   (eggs, seeds, adults)

3. The male part of flowers makes tiny grains called _____.
   (seeds, pollen, conifers)

4. Conifers make male _____ that hold pollen.
   (cones, flowers, roots)

5. Conifers make seeds in their _____ cones.
   (fruit, male, female)

## B. Draw a line to complete each sentence.

1. Female parts of flowering plants        make male and female cones.

2. Conifers        make eggs.

3. Male parts of flowering plants        make pollen.

## C. Write one or more sentences to answer the question.

Squirrels eat seeds such as those found in nuts like acorns. How do squirrels help seeds grow?

_____
_____
_____
_____

19

# CHAPTER 1

# Watch a Plant in Action

## You need:

- cup
- spoon
- water
- red or blue food coloring
- celery with leaves
- notepaper

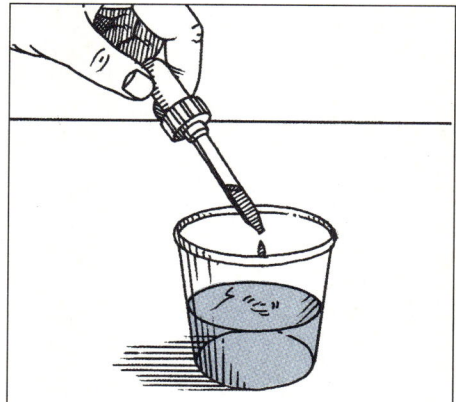

**In this activity you will see how water moves through a plant.**

Follow these steps:

1. Fill a cup about one-half full of water. Add ten drops of food coloring. Stir the water with a spoon.

2. Put the celery in the water. Wait four hours and then observe the celery. Write what happened on your notepaper.

3. Take the celery out of the water. Peel open the celery to look at the inside. Write what you see.

**Write answers to these questions.**

1. What happened to the water in the cup? How can you tell?

   _____
   _____
   _____

2. How does water move through a plant?

   _____
   _____
   _____

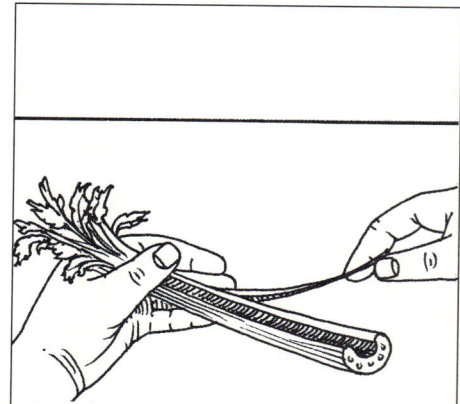

# TEST CHAPTER 1

**Darken the circle next to the correct answer.**

1. What are the three main parts of plants?
   - Ⓐ stems, leaves, and cells
   - Ⓑ leaves, trunks, and branches
   - Ⓒ roots, stems, and leaves
   - Ⓓ soil, roots, and stems

2. What part of a plant is the trunk of a tree?
   - Ⓐ root
   - Ⓑ stem
   - Ⓒ leaf
   - Ⓓ stomata

3. All living things are made of
   - Ⓐ carbon dioxide.
   - Ⓑ leaves.
   - Ⓒ plants.
   - Ⓓ cells.

4. You need a microscope to see most cells because they are very
   - Ⓐ dark.
   - Ⓑ bright.
   - Ⓒ large.
   - Ⓓ small.

5. Plants make food using a process called
   - Ⓐ photosynthesis.
   - Ⓑ chlorophyll.
   - Ⓒ carbon dioxide.
   - Ⓓ oxygen.

6. What gas do plants use to make food?
   - Ⓐ oxygen
   - Ⓑ carbon dioxide
   - Ⓒ chlorophyll
   - Ⓓ photosynthesis

7. In a plant, what moves through phloem?
   - Ⓐ food
   - Ⓑ water
   - Ⓒ nutrients
   - Ⓓ stomata

8. The leaves and stems of a plant grow toward
   - Ⓐ light.
   - Ⓑ darkness.
   - Ⓒ the center of Earth.
   - Ⓓ the leaves of other plants.

9. When can a plant reproduce?
   - Ⓐ anytime
   - Ⓑ birth
   - Ⓒ adulthood
   - Ⓓ death

10. What kinds of plants make seeds inside cones?
    - Ⓐ conifers
    - Ⓑ xylem
    - Ⓒ flowering plants
    - Ⓓ pollen

# CHAPTER 2

# How Animals Live and Grow

Riding on its parent's feet protects this emperor penguin chick from the cold, icy ground. The parent and the chick don't look very much alike now, but they have many things in common. They walk and swim. They need food to live. And the chick will grow up to look a lot like its parents. In this chapter you will learn how animals are alike and different in how they live and grow.

**What is it?**

- It covers the outside of a grasshopper.
- You do not have one.
- It is like a hard shell.

LESSON

# What Are Animals?

Like plants, all animals are living things made of many cells. Animals can reproduce, and they need food and water to live. But animals are also alike in some ways that make them different from plants. For example, animals can't make their own food. They must eat plants or other animals. Most animals can move from place to place. Animals move for many reasons, such as to find food, water, and new places to live.

All animals have different parts called **organs**. Organs are made up of different kinds of tissue that work together to do different jobs. Stomachs and brains are organs. So is **skin**. The skin's job is to protect an animal's body. Many animals also have bones. Bones are organs that make up the **skeleton**. The skeleton is a frame that holds up an animal's body.

There are many kinds of animals. Animals come in many different shapes and sizes. They may have different kinds of organs. They may live in different ways. Some animals have bones down the middle of their backs. Others do not. Some have six legs, or even more. Others have no legs at all. Different animals are covered with skin, fur, feathers, or shells. Some can live only on dry land. Others must stay underwater. A few animals are huge. The biggest is the blue whale. It can grow to be one hundred feet long. Animals can be tiny, too. Mites are tiny animals. Some mites are only as big as the period at the end of this sentence. Other mites are even smaller. You need a microscope to see them.

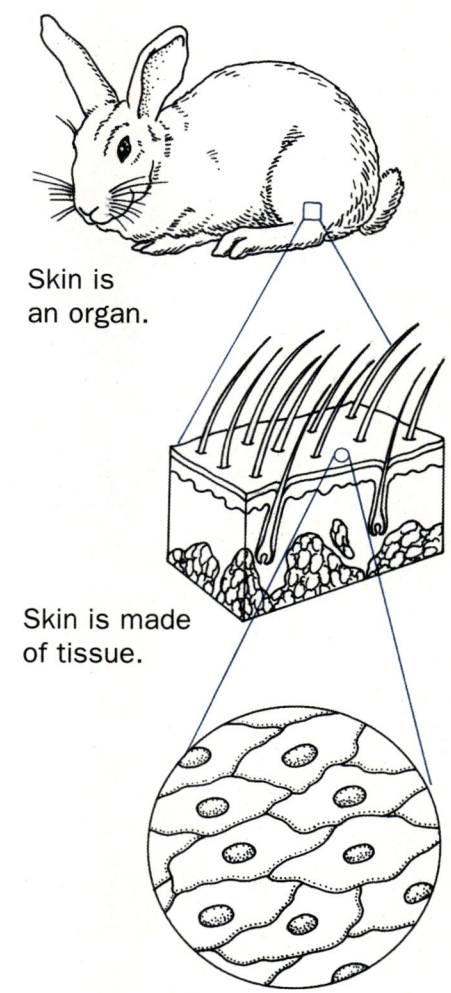

Skin is an organ.

Skin is made of tissue.

Tissue is made of cells.

## A. Write True if the sentence is true. Write False if the sentence is false.

_____ 1. Unlike plants, animals cannot reproduce.

_____ 2. All animals can make their own food.

_____ 3. Most animals can move from place to place to find what they need.

_____ 4. All animals have the same kinds of organs.

_____ 5. The biggest animal is the blue whale.

_____ 6. Some animals are so small that you need a microscope to see them.

## B. Write the missing word or words in each sentence.

1. Both plants and animals are made of _____.
   (skin, cells, bones)

2. All animals have different _____ that do different jobs.
   (skeletons, legs, organs)

3. One kind of organ is _____.
   (tissue, a cell, the skin)

4. Some animals have frames called _____ that hold up their bodies.
   (skin, skeletons, feathers)

## C. Write one or more sentences to answer the question.

As animals, what are four ways that whales and mites are alike?

_____
_____
_____
_____

# LESSON 2 How Are Animals Grouped?

Scientists put living things into groups. You already have learned about plant groups, such as flowering plants and conifers. Animals have different groups, too.

There are many ways to group animals. For example, animals that live on land form a group. Humans and grasshoppers are land animals. Animals that live in water form another group. Fish and whales are water animals.

There are other ways to sort animals. For example, some animals are **cold-blooded**. The temperature inside a cold-blooded animal's body changes with the temperature outside. Grasshoppers and snakes are cold-blooded. When they are cold, they move less often and more slowly. They may lie in the sun to warm up. When they are warm, they move faster. If they get too hot, they will cool off in a shady spot. Other animals are **warm-blooded**. The temperature inside their bodies always stays about the same. Humans and whales are both warm-blooded. They act in about the same way whether it is hot or cold outside their bodies.

Another way to group animals is by body parts. For example, animals that have skeletons with a backbone are called **vertebrates**. Humans, whales, and fish are vertebrates. Animals that do not have backbones are called **invertebrates**. A grasshopper is an invertebrate. It does not have any bones inside its body. Instead, its skeleton covers its body on the outside. It is called an **exoskeleton** and is like a hard shell.

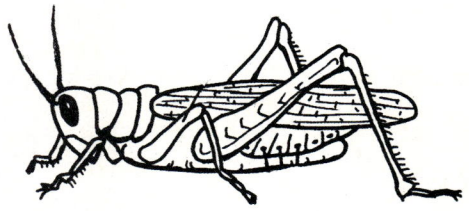
Grasshoppers are invertebrates. They do not have backbones.

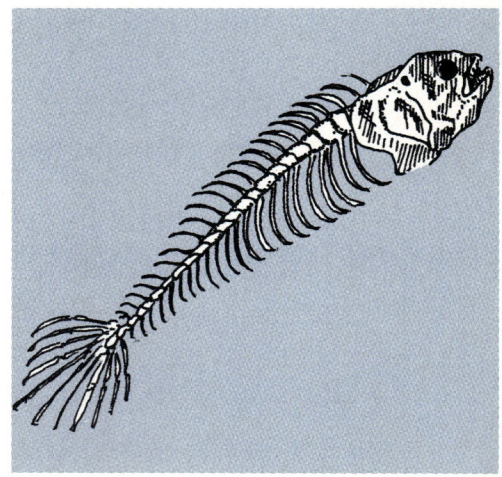
Fish are vertebrates. They have skeletons with backbones.

## A.

Put a ✔ in the correct box after the name of each animal.

| Animal | Land animal | Water animal |
|---|---|---|
| 1. human | | |
| 2. grasshopper | | |
| 3. whale | | |
| 4. fish | | |

## B.

Put a ✔ in the correct box after the name of each animal.

| Animal | Warm-blooded | Cold-blooded |
|---|---|---|
| 1. human | | |
| 2. grasshopper | | |
| 3. whale | | |
| 4. fish | | |

## C.

Put a ✔ in the correct box after the name of each animal.

| Animal | Vertebrate | Invertebrate |
|---|---|---|
| 1. human | | |
| 2. grasshopper | | |
| 3. whale | | |
| 4. fish | | |

## D.

**Write answers to these questions.**

This picture shows the skeleton of a bird that makes its nest in trees and eats worms and bugs. It behaves about the same in cold weather as it does in warm weather.

1. Is the bird a land animal or a water animal?
   _____

2. Is the bird warm-blooded or cold-blooded?
   _____

3. Is the bird a vertebrate or an invertebrate?
   _____

# LESSON 3: How Do Animals Use Oxygen, Water, and Food?

Animals need three main things to live. They need oxygen, water, and food. All animals must breathe oxygen. Oxygen helps give the body energy to live and grow. Fish get oxygen from water. You get oxygen from the air around you.

Animals also need water to live. In fact, most of your body is made of water. Your body is about two-thirds water. Most of that water is in your cells. More than half of your blood is water. Your blood carries oxygen, water, and food to all parts of your body.

You need to drink plenty of water to stay healthy. Some foods have water in them. Apples and oranges have a lot of water in them. When you eat an apple, your body uses the water in it.

Animals also need energy from food to live and grow. To get energy from food, your body must **digest** it, or break it down. Digestion begins in your mouth. Your teeth break food into small pieces. The pieces then move down into your **stomach**. Your stomach mixes the food with special materials that turn it into a soupy liquid.

From your stomach, the soupy liquid food moves into your **intestines**, which are like long tubes. The food has been broken into such tiny bits that it can soak through your intestines and into your blood. Your blood then carries the food and water to every cell in your body. In your cells, food and oxygen act together to give your body the energy it needs to move, grow, and repair itself.

**Digesting Food**

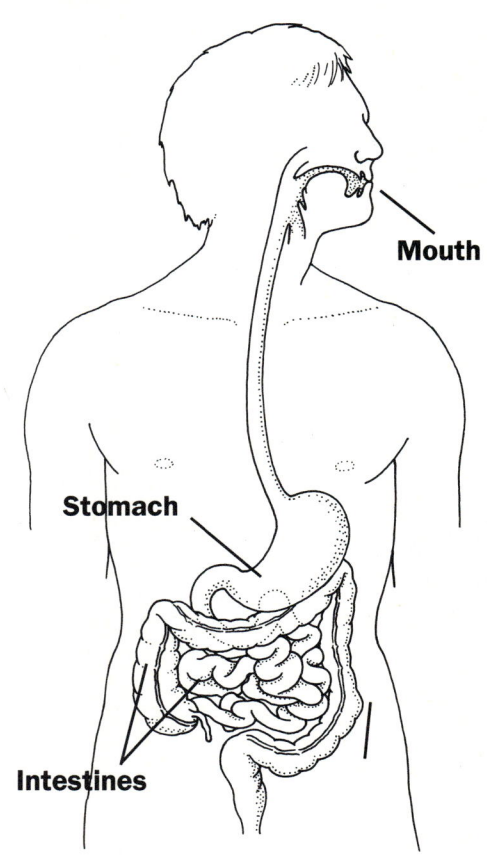

**A.** **Underline the correct word in each sentence.**

1. Three main things all animals need are oxygen, water, and (sunlight, skeletons, **food**).

2. Humans get the (**oxygen**, water, food) they need from the air around them.

3. Your body is about (**two-thirds**, one-half, one-fourth) water.

4. To get energy from food, your body must (make, breathe, **digest**) it.

5. Blood carries (**food**, cells, intestines) through the body.

**B.** **Write mouth, stomach, or intestines to tell where each action takes place.**

1. Food and water move into the blood. _____

2. Teeth break food into small pieces. _____

3. Food is turned into a soupy liquid. _____

**C.** **Write one or more sentences to answer the questions.**

1. Some animals that live in deserts never drink water. How do you think they get the water they need?

   _____
   _____
   _____
   _____

2. You are a scientist looking for a planet where animals might live. What things do you look for? Why?

   _____
   _____
   _____
   _____

## LESSON 4: How Do Animals Change?

Like plants, all animals have life cycles. Different animals have different kinds of life cycles. Most life cycles have things in common. For example, all animals begin as eggs. Some animals, such as birds and fish, lay eggs outside their bodies. In the eggs, baby animals grow until they are strong enough to be born and live outside the egg. Other animals, like rabbits and horses, keep eggs inside their bodies. The eggs develop into babies there. When animals are born, the first stage of their life cycle is over.

The second part of an animal's life cycle comes after birth. During this time, many young animals are helpless and need their parents to feed them and keep them safe. For example, baby birds cannot fly. Their parents bring them food. Other animals do not need their parents. They can find food by themselves. For example, fish can swim and find food as soon as they are born.

During the third part of the life cycle, animals grow larger and stronger. They change as they grow into adults. Young birds learn to fly. Young fish get stronger and swim farther. During this part of their life cycles, animals cannot reproduce.

In the final part of the life cycle, animals are adults. Adult animals are able to reproduce. When they reproduce, they make new animals. These new animals also have life cycles. When the adult animal dies, it leaves living children behind. The children grow up to be adults. Then, they have their own children. This cycle keeps repeating itself over and over again.

### Life Cycle of a Rabbit

New rabbits develop from eggs inside their mother.

The mother feeds baby rabbits with milk.

Young rabbits eat plants. When they are adults, they will be able to reproduce.

**A.** Write <u>True</u> if the sentence is true. Write <u>False</u> if the sentence is false.

_____ 1. All living things have life cycles.

_____ 2. All animals start their life cycles as adults.

_____ 3. Horses develop inside their mothers' bodies.

_____ 4. The second part of an animal's life cycle comes before birth.

_____ 5. Unlike young animals, adults can reproduce.

**B.** The sentences below tell about a rabbit's life cycle. Write 1, 2, 3, and 4 to show the correct order.

_____ The rabbit becomes an adult and can reproduce.

_____ The mother feeds the baby.

_____ An egg develops inside the mother.

_____ The young rabbit grows but cannot yet reproduce.

**C.** The sentences below tell about a bird's life cycle. Write 1, 2, 3, and 4 to show the correct order.

_____ The young bird cannot fly and is fed by its parents.

_____ The bird becomes an adult and can reproduce.

_____ The young bird learns to fly.

_____ An egg develops in a nest.

**D.** Write one or more sentences to answer the question.

How are the life cycles of fish, birds, and rabbits alike and different?

_____

_____

_____

_____

_____

# LESSON 5
## How Do People Grow and Change?

Humans have life cycles, just as other living things do. Humans are **mammals**. Mammals are animals that have hair and feed their young with milk. Like other mammals, humans start their life cycles as eggs inside their mothers. They grow and develop there for about nine months.

After birth, human babies are helpless. They need a lot of care. They need to be fed and kept warm and safe. Babies must also be held, cuddled, and talked to. Otherwise, they may not develop or grow well.

Over time, babies grow and change. They come to look more like adults as their bodies grow bigger and their arms and legs get longer. During this time, they are called children. They can talk and walk and do some things that adults do. However, children are not able to reproduce.

As children develop, they become taller and stronger. Not all children grow at the same speed. Some children may be shorter than their friends one year. Two years later, they may catch up or be taller than their friends.

Babies and young children learn many things very quickly. They learn to walk and run. They learn all about the world and people around them. As children develop, they are able to learn more facts, skills, and ideas.

Humans reach the next stage of their life cycles when they become adults. Adults are able to reproduce. Human adults still change as they grow older. But they usually change more slowly than when they were babies and children.

**Life Cycle of a Human**

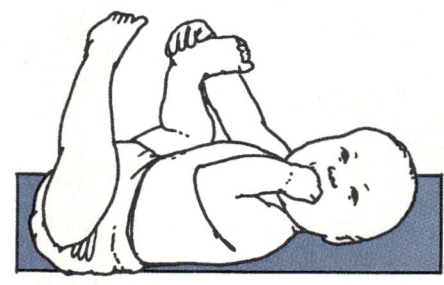
Baby

Child

Adult

## A. Write the word that best completes each sentence.

adults    babies    grow    inside    mammals

1. Humans are _____, animals that feed their babies with milk.

2. Humans start as eggs that grow _____ their mothers' bodies.

3. Just after humans are born, they are called _____.

4. When humans are _____, they change more slowly than when they were children.

5. Children's bodies do not all _____ at the same speed.

## B. Write a sentence that tells about each of these parts of a human's life cycle.

1. baby _____

_____

2. child _____

_____

3. adult _____

_____

## C. Write one or more sentences to answer the question.

What part of the life cycle are you in now?

_____

_____

# LESSON 6

# What Are Characteristics?

Animals usually look like their parents. For example, a young grasshopper grows up to be an adult grasshopper. A young grasshopper has many things in common with its parents. It has six legs and a hard exoskeleton. It jumps through the air and eats plants. We say that these are the **characteristics** of grasshoppers.

Grasshoppers do not choose to have six legs or an exoskeleton. They do not learn to jump through the air or eat plants. Grasshoppers **inherit**, or get, these characteristics from their parents. Characteristics like these are passed down from parents to children.

Humans are also like their parents. Many children look like their parents in some ways. They may have long or short legs like their parents. A child may have a turned-up nose like her father or freckles like her mother. Children may have the same eye color and hair color as their parents. Children inherit these characteristics from their parents.

However, humans do not inherit all of their characteristics from their parents. Often, humans learn new characteristics. For example, you may know how to play the piano. So, one of your characteristics is being able to play the piano. You did not inherit this characteristic from your parents, even if they know how to play the piano. Instead, you learned how to do this. Characteristics that are learned are not passed down from parents to children.

Hair color is an inherited characteristic. Being able to skate is a learned characteristic.

## A. Write the missing word or words in each sentence.

1. A characteristic that a grasshopper shares with its parents is _____.
   (a life cycle, a hard exoskeleton, four legs)

2. Brown eyes are a characteristic that children _____ their parents.
   (inherit from, learn from, pass on to)

3. Knowing how to read and write is a characteristic that is _____.
   (inherited, learned, passed down)

## B. Write <u>inherited</u> or <u>learned</u> to tell how a person gets each characteristic.

1. Playing the violin _____
2. Having blue eyes _____
3. Riding a bicycle _____
4. Having curly hair _____
5. Having small ears _____

## C. Write one or more sentences to answer the questions.

1. What is a characteristic that a child can inherit from his or her parents?

   _____
   _____
   _____

2. What is one characteristic that you have learned?

   _____
   _____
   _____

CHAPTER 2

# Watch Animals in Action

**You need:**

- fish tank or fish bowl with fish
- fish food
- paper
- pencil
- ruler

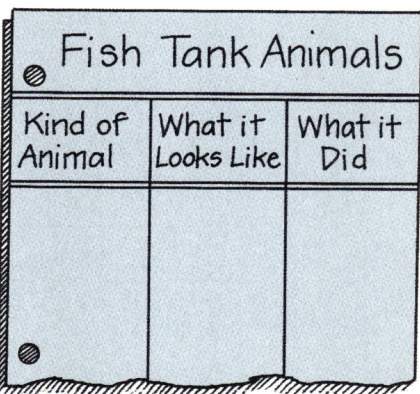

**In this activity you will observe animals—fish in a fish tank.**

Follow these steps:

1. Make a chart like the one shown.

2. Put some fish food in the fish tank. Observe the animals for about 15 minutes. Notice what they do and how they move.

3. Write your findings on your chart. Use your chart to tell what the animals do.

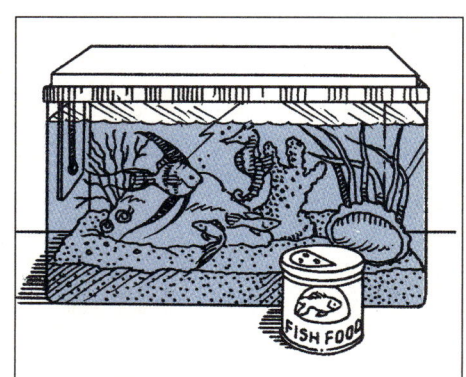

**Write answers to these questions.**

1. How do the animals get food and water?

   _____
   _____
   _____

2. How do you think the animals get oxygen?

   _____
   _____

3. What was the most interesting thing you saw? What made it so interesting?

   _____
   _____

# TEST CHAPTER 2

**Darken the circle next to the correct answer.**

1. What is something that all animals have?
   - Ⓐ bones
   - Ⓑ cells
   - Ⓒ skin
   - Ⓓ legs

2. Skin, bones, and brains are kinds of
   - Ⓐ cells.
   - Ⓑ organs.
   - Ⓒ skeletons.
   - Ⓓ exoskeletons.

3. Animals whose body temperatures change with the temperature outside are called
   - Ⓐ cold-blooded animals.
   - Ⓑ water animals.
   - Ⓒ warm-blooded animals.
   - Ⓓ land animals.

4. Vertebrates are animals that have
   - Ⓐ skin.
   - Ⓑ legs.
   - Ⓒ exoskeletons.
   - Ⓓ backbones.

5. What three main things do animals need to live?
   - Ⓐ carbon dioxide, water, and food
   - Ⓑ oxygen, sunlight, and water
   - Ⓒ sunlight, water, and food
   - Ⓓ oxygen, water, and food

6. What must your body do to get energy from food?
   - Ⓐ make it
   - Ⓑ digest it
   - Ⓒ repair it
   - Ⓓ grow it

7. Where does a human egg grow?
   - Ⓐ in a nest
   - Ⓑ outside its mother's body
   - Ⓒ inside its mother's body
   - Ⓓ in pond water

8. What are the stages of the human life cycle?
   - Ⓐ egg, cell, child, adult
   - Ⓑ seed, baby, child, adult
   - Ⓒ egg, baby, child, adult
   - Ⓓ baby, egg, child, adult

9. Being able to play the violin is a characteristic that children
   - Ⓐ take.
   - Ⓑ grow.
   - Ⓒ inherit.
   - Ⓓ learn.

10. Hair color is a characteristic that people inherit from their
    - Ⓐ parents.
    - Ⓑ children.
    - Ⓒ friends.
    - Ⓓ brothers and sisters.

# CHAPTER 3

# Your Senses

Most animals, including people, stay away from skunks. That's because skunks produce a very strong smell. What other senses do you use to learn about the world? How do you learn about the shape and color of the skunk? How do you learn what the skunk sounds like when it walks through the woods? In this chapter you will learn how your senses tell you about the world around you.

## What is it?

- It is part of the ear.
- It is full of liquid.
- It is shaped like a snail.

## LESSON 1: How Can You Learn About the World?

You use your senses to learn about the world around you. You have the senses of **sight**, **hearing**, **smell**, **taste**, and **touch**. Together, these senses help you see, hear, smell, taste, and feel the world around you.

Your body has special cells that can sense different things such as colors, sounds, smells, and tastes. These cells are called **receptor cells**. Different kinds of receptor cells can sense different kinds of things. For example, receptor cells in your eyes sense colors and light. There are also many receptor cells in your skin. When you pick up an object such as a pencil, receptor cells in your fingertips sense the pencil against your skin. You have receptor cells like these all over your body.

Receptor cells are in special organs called **sense organs**. Your eyes, ears, tongue, nose, and skin are your sense organs. Sense organs send signals about the outside world to your brain. The signals move from the sense organs through thousands of **nerve cells**. Nerve cells form pathways between sense organs and your brain. These pathways of nerve cells, together with the brain, make up what is called the **nervous system**.

Your senses help you enjoy food, sound, and color. They keep you from hurting yourself. For example, your lips can sense high temperatures. They send signals to the brain when you are about to drink something that is too hot. Your brain then warns you to wait until the liquid is cool enough to drink. Without your senses, you could hurt yourself and not even know it.

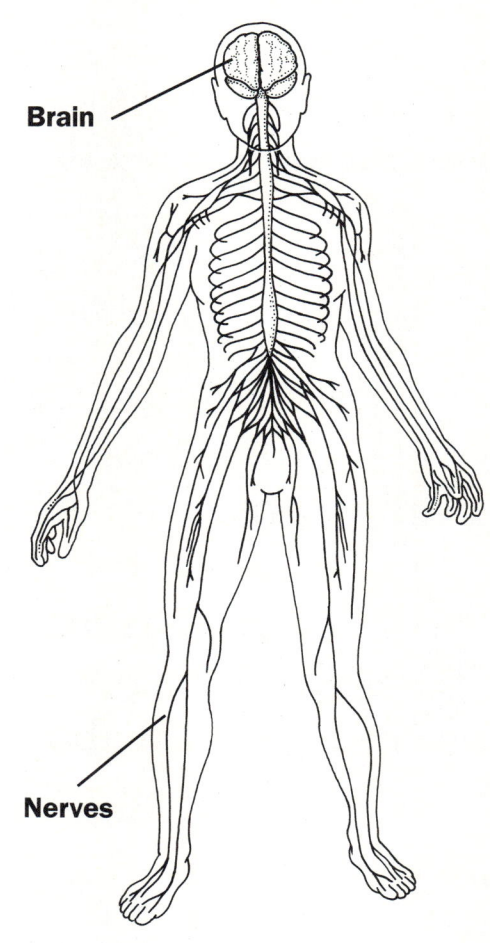

**The Nervous System**

Brain

Nerves

## A. Write the missing word or words in each sentence.

1. The five senses are sight, hearing, taste, _____.

   (smell, and touch; ears, and eyes; mouth, and smell)

2. Cells that can sense color and sound are called _____.

   (sense organs, receptor cells, nervous system)

3. Your eyes, ears, tongue, and nose are _____.
   (receptor cells, sense organs, senses)

4. Sense organs send signals about the outside world to the _____.

   (receptor cells, senses, brain)

5. Nerve cells and the brain make up the _____.
   (receptor cells, sense organs, nervous system)

## B. The sentences below tell how your sense of hearing works. Write 1, 2, and 3 to show the correct order of these events.

_____ A signal reaches the brain.

_____ Receptor cells in the ears hear some music.

_____ A signal moves through nerve cells.

## C. Write one or more sentences to answer the question.

How could your sense of smell protect you from danger?

_____
_____
_____
_____

# LESSON 2
## How Do the Eyes Work?

The eyes are the sense organs of sight. The eye has four main parts—the **pupil**, **iris**, **lens**, and **retina**. These parts work together to sense light and colors and send signals to the brain.

The **pupil** is the black circle in the center of your eye. It is a hole that lets light into your eye. The **iris** is the colored part of your eye. The pupil is in the iris. Muscles in the iris work to change the size of the pupil. The iris gets bigger in bright light. As the iris gets bigger, the pupil gets smaller. In very bright light, the pupil can get as small as the head of a pin. When the pupil gets smaller, less light reaches the inside of the eye. In very dim light, the iris gets smaller and the pupil gets bigger. As the pupil gets bigger, more light reaches the inside of the eye.

The **lens** of the eye is behind the pupil. The lens bends the light so that it forms a picture on the **retina**. The retina is a layer of tissue at the back of the eye. It covers about two-thirds of the back of the eye. The retina has millions of receptor cells.

There are two kinds of receptor cells in the retina, **rods** and **cones**. Rods sense dim light. Cones sense bright light and colors. Rods and cones change the light that you see into signals for the brain.

Each of your eyes has an **optic nerve**. The optic nerve is the pathway that carries signals from the rods and cones to the brain. The brain uses the signals from both optic nerves to form one picture.

**Parts of the Eye**

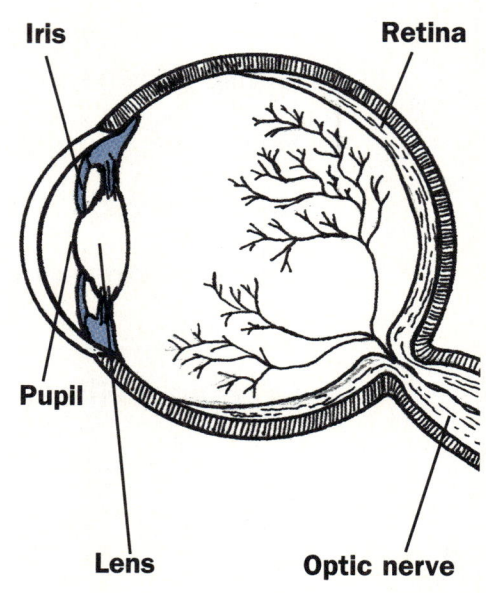

## A. Write the word that best completes each sentence.

iris    lens    less    light    pupil    receptor

1. The pupil, iris, _____, and retina are main parts of the eye.

2. Light enters the eye through the _____.

3. The colored part of the eye is the _____.

4. When the pupil is small, _____ light gets into the eye.

5. The lens bends the _____ so that it reaches the retina.

6. The eye's _____ cells are in the retina.

## B. Write <u>rods</u>, <u>cones</u>, or <u>both</u> to answer each question.

1. Which cells are receptor cells in the retina? _____

2. Which cells sense dim light? _____

3. Which cells sense colors? _____

## C. Write one or more sentences to answer the questions.

Some people cannot see well at night because parts of their eyes do not work well. Which part of the eye is most likely not working? Why do you think so?

_____
_____
_____
_____
_____

43

## LESSON 3

# How Do the Ears Work?

The ears are the sense organs of hearing. Ears have receptor cells that sense sound and send signals about the sound to the brain.

The three main parts of the ear are the **outer ear**, the **middle ear**, and the **inner ear**. The outer ear is the part of the ear you can see. The middle ear and inner ear are inside your head.

Sound moving through the air reaches your outer ear first. The outer ear guides the sound toward the **eardrum**. The eardrum is a piece of tissue that is pulled tightly like the top of a drum. It is a little smaller than a dime. The eardrum is the last part of the outer ear.

On the other side of the eardrum is the middle ear. Inside the middle ear are three tiny bones. When sound reaches the eardrum, it moves the eardrum back and forth. When the eardrum moves back and forth, the three tiny bones in the middle ear also move back and forth. The tiny bones pass the motion of the sound from the outer ear to the inner ear.

Inside the inner ear is the **cochlea**, which is shaped like a snail. The cochlea has tubes filled with liquid. There are tiny hairs in the tubes that lead to the ear's receptor cells. When the bones of the middle ear move, waves form in the liquid of the cochlea. As the waves pass over the tiny hairs, the receptor cells change the motion of the waves into signals for the brain. The signals move from the receptor cells in the cochlea along a nerve to the brain.

**Parts of the Ear**

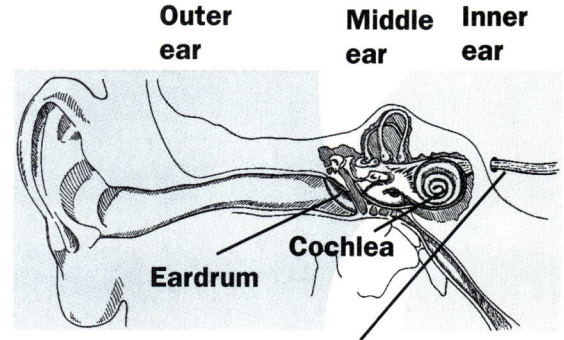

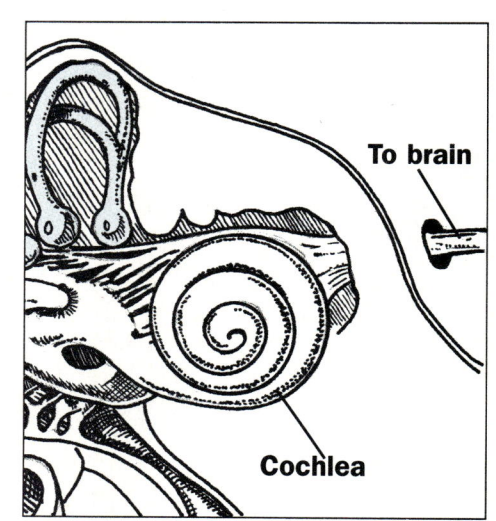

## A. Write True if the sentence is true. Write False if the sentence is false.

_____ 1. You can clearly see all three main parts of the ear.

_____ 2. The eardrum is between the middle ear and the inner ear.

_____ 3. The cochlea has tubes filled with liquid.

## B. Write the missing word or words in each sentence.

1. Three tiny bones pass the motion of sound to the _____ ear.

   (outer, middle, inner)

2. The cochlea has tiny hairs that lead to the ear's _____.

   (tiny bones, receptor cells, eardrum)

3. Receptor cells change the motion of waves into signals for the _____.

   (eardrum, middle ear, brain)

## C. Write outer ear, middle ear, or inner ear to tell where each of the following can be found.

1. cochlea _____

2. three tiny bones _____

3. eardrum _____

## D. Write one or more sentences to answer the questions.

Not all sounds make the same number of hairs in the cochlea move. What kinds of sounds do you think make more hairs move? What kinds of sounds make fewer hairs move?

_____

_____

_____

# LESSON 4
## How Do Taste and Smell Work?

Your tongue and nose are sense organs. They have receptor cells that sense tastes and smells. These cells send signals about tastes and smells to your brain.

The receptor cells for taste are in the **taste buds** on your tongue. Taste buds have receptor cells that sense four different tastes—sweet, salty, sour, and bitter. Once the taste buds sense a taste, they send a signal to your brain. Your brain tells you what you are tasting.

Your sense of smell picks up **odors**. Odors are smells in the air. As air passes through the nose, odors pass over receptor cells. These receptor cells are called **olfactory cells**. If there is enough of the odor in the air, the olfactory cells send a signal to your brain. Your brain tells you what you are smelling. The brain can sense about ten thousand different smells.

The sense of smell normally works along with your sense of taste. Think of a time when you had a cold or a stuffy nose. You may have noticed that your food didn't taste very good. Even your favorite foods seemed to lose their taste. This is because your brain uses information both from your sense of smell and sense of taste to tell one food from another. Without your sense of smell, your sense of taste does not seem to work as well.

You can prove this to yourself. Hold your nose. Then, eat some food, such as a piece of fruit. You'll find that the fruit has very little taste when you are holding your nose.

### The Sense of Smell

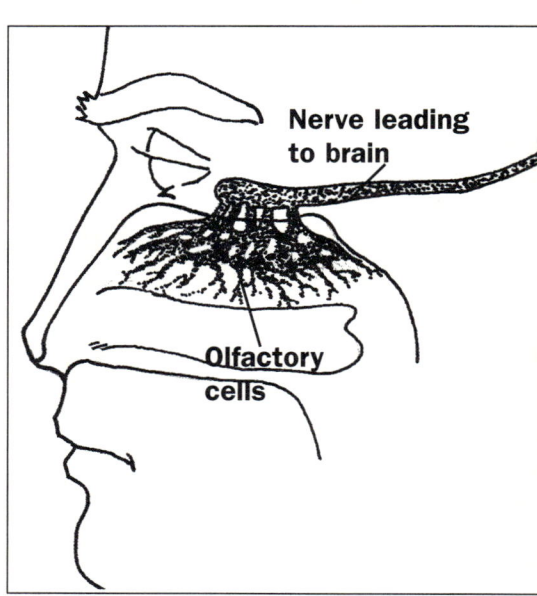

If you hold your nose while eating, food will have less taste.

## A. Write the word or words that best complete each sentence.

odors          salty          taste buds
olfactory cells     taste     tongue

1. Your nose and your _____ are both sense organs.

2. Your tongue has receptor cells for taste in the _____.

3. Taste buds in your tongue can sense sweet, sour, _____, and bitter.

4. The air carries _____ that are sensed by cells in your nose.

5. The receptor cells in your nose are called _____.

6. Your sense of smell helps you _____ foods.

## B. Write True if the sentence is true. Write False if the sentence is false.

_____ 1. Olfactory cells send signals to the taste buds.

_____ 2. Taste buds pick up smells in the air called odors.

_____ 3. Food has less taste if you hold your nose while you eat.

## C. Write one or more sentences to answer the question.

How can your sense of taste protect you?

_____

_____

_____

# LESSON 5

## What Is Touch?

Skin is an important sense organ. Skin lets us know touch. There are tiny nerves just beneath your skin. These tiny nerves are your skin's receptor cells.

Skin has different kinds of receptor cells. Each kind of receptor cell senses only one kind of feeling. Cold receptor cells sense anything that is colder than your skin. Heat receptor cells sense anything that is hotter than your skin. **Pressure** receptor cells sense when something is touching your skin. Deep pressure receptor cells sense when something is pushing against your skin. Pain receptor cells sense when something hurts.

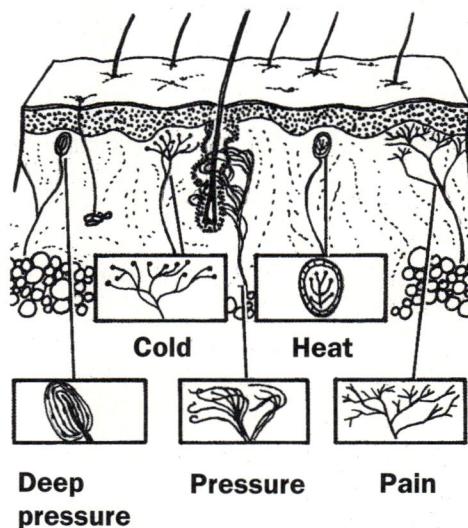

**Receptor Cells in Skin**

Cold  Heat

Deep pressure  Pressure  Pain

The receptor cells send signals that move through the pathways in the nervous system to the brain. Your brain then tells you what you are feeling. It helps you tell the difference between fur and sand. It also helps you tell the difference between something that is wet and something that is dry.

There are more receptor cells on some parts of the body than on others. For example, there are many receptor cells in your fingertips and the inside of your wrist. The back of your neck has fewer receptor cells.

Some pain receptor cells are inside your body. These receptor cells can send signals to your brain, too. For example, pain receptors in your throat let you know when you have a sore throat. Pain receptors in your stomach let you know when you have a stomachache.

The inside of the wrist has a lot of receptor cells.

**A.** Write the names of the kinds of receptor cells found just beneath your skin.

1. _____
2. _____
3. _____
4. _____
5. _____

**B.** Write <u>Yes</u> if the sentence tells what the receptor cells in your skin can do. Write <u>No</u> if the sentence tells something the receptor cells cannot do.

_____ 1. They can tell the difference between salty and sour.

_____ 2. They can tell the difference between light and dark.

_____ 3. They can tell the difference between rough and smooth.

_____ 4. They can tell the difference between spoiled milk and perfume.

_____ 5. They can tell the difference between cold and hot.

**C.** Write one or more sentences to answer the question.

Why do you think the mother is testing the temperature of the baby's milk on her own wrist?

_____
_____
_____
_____
_____

## LESSON 6

# How Can You Protect Your Senses?

Your senses can help keep you away from danger. For example, you see a banana peel on the sidewalk and walk around it. You hear a train coming and stay away from the railroad tracks. You smell smoke and escape a fire.

To keep you away from danger, your senses and your nervous system need to be healthy. There are many things you can do to keep your senses and nervous system healthy. Eating the right kinds of foods is a good start. Exercise and rest are important, too. They help keep your nervous system working the way it should.

You can protect your nervous system by wearing a helmet and pads.

You can protect your hearing by staying away from loud noises. Sunglasses can protect your eyes from bright sunlight. You can protect your brain by wearing a helmet when you ride a bike, skateboard, or in-line skate. You can also protect your skin by keeping it from getting sunburned.

There are some things that harm your nervous system. For example, smoking can harm your sense of taste and your sense of smell. Drinking too much alcohol can harm your vision. It can also slow the signals that move through your nervous system.

There may be times when you do not feel well. Your doctor may give you **prescription drugs**, medicine to help you feel better. Be sure to follow the doctor's directions. Take the prescription only when your doctor tells you. Prescription drugs help you get well. But they hurt your body and your nervous system if you take them when you are well.

**A.** Write the missing word or words in each sentence.

1. The right foods will keep your nervous system _____.
   (healthy, slow, in danger)

2. Loud noises can harm your _____.
   (sight, hearing, taste buds)

3. Alcohol can slow down the _____ in your nervous system.
   (signals, drugs, noises)

4. Prescription drugs can help your body if you take them _____.
   (all the time, when the doctor says you should, when you want them)

**B.** Write <u>Yes</u> if the word or words describe something that is good for your nervous system. Write <u>No</u> if the word or words describe something that is harmful to your nervous system.

1. bike helmet _____
2. rest _____
3. exercise _____
4. alcohol _____
5. loud noises _____

**C.** Write one or more sentences to answer the question.

What part or parts of your ears might be damaged by loud noises?

_____
_____
_____
_____

# CHAPTER 3

## Use Your Sense of Touch

**You need:**

- paper bags of mystery objects
- paper
- pencil

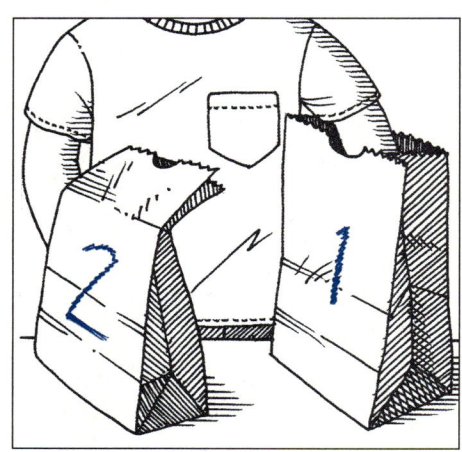

**In this activity you will use only your sense of touch to name things that are in a paper bag.**

Follow these steps:

1. Begin by putting one hand into the bag. Don't take anything out of the bag. Don't peek into the bag. Touch what is in the bag very carefully. Is it soft? Is it hard? Is it small? Is it big?

2. List each thing you think is in the bag. Then, follow the same steps with each of the other bags. Write what you learn by using only your sense of touch.

3. After you have tested all the bags, look inside them. Were you able to correctly name the things in each bag?

**Write answers to these questions.**

1. What did your sense of touch tell you about the things in the bags?

2. What other senses could you use to learn about the objects in the bags?

# TEST  CHAPTER 3

**Darken the circle next to the correct answer.**

1. The five senses are sight, hearing, taste, smell, and
   - Ⓐ skin.
   - Ⓑ touch.
   - Ⓒ nerves.
   - Ⓓ light.

2. What are the cells that can sense things such as heat, color, and pain called?
   - Ⓐ senses
   - Ⓑ receptor cells
   - Ⓒ retinas
   - Ⓓ nervous system

3. The pupil, iris, lens, and retina are parts of the
   - Ⓐ eye.
   - Ⓑ ear.
   - Ⓒ nose.
   - Ⓓ nervous system.

4. Signals from your rods and cones travel to your brain along the
   - Ⓐ pupil.
   - Ⓑ lens.
   - Ⓒ iris.
   - Ⓓ optic nerve.

5. The cochlea holds the receptor cells for
   - Ⓐ sight.
   - Ⓑ hearing.
   - Ⓒ touch.
   - Ⓓ taste.

6. Which tastes can your taste buds sense?
   - Ⓐ heat, cold, pain, pressure
   - Ⓑ iris, pupil, lens, retina
   - Ⓒ sweet, salty, sour, bitter
   - Ⓓ sight, hearing, smell, touch

7. What sense uses olfactory cells?
   - Ⓐ sight
   - Ⓑ hearing
   - Ⓒ smell
   - Ⓓ touch

8. Which sense helps you know the difference between soft and rough and hot and cold?
   - Ⓐ hearing
   - Ⓑ touch
   - Ⓒ smell
   - Ⓓ taste

9. The receptor cells in skin are
   - Ⓐ sweet, salty, and bitter.
   - Ⓑ sight, hearing, and taste.
   - Ⓒ hot, cold, pain, pressure, and deep pressure.
   - Ⓓ iris, pupil, lens, and retina.

10. What are some things you can do to protect your senses?
    - Ⓐ drink alcohol
    - Ⓑ smoke, wear sunglasses
    - Ⓒ take prescription drugs, listen to loud music
    - Ⓓ eat right, exercise, wear a bike helmet

# Careers

## Horticulturist

*Hortus* means garden. A horticulturist is a kind of gardener. Horticulturists grow plants, such as fruits, vegetables, and flowers. They also find better ways to take care of plants. Sometimes horticulturists mix two kinds of plants together to grow a new plant. The new plant might be stronger or have fruit that tastes better than that of other plants. Or it might have flowers that are unusual and beautiful.

## Entomologist

How do bees make honey? What do beetles eat? To find out, you could ask an entomologist. An entomologist studies insects, as well as spiders, ticks, mites, and centipedes. Learning about insects helps entomologists solve problems. They find ways to stop insects from eating a farmer's crops. They also develop ways to protect insects, such as bees, that help people.

## Pharmacist

When people are sick, sometimes they need medicine to help them get better. Doctors can tell people what kind of medicine they need. A pharmacist prepares the medicine.

Pharmacists have to make sure that the medicine they give to people is safe. They use very clean tools and measure the medicine carefully. They also check their work to make sure that they have not made any mistakes.

# Unit 2
# Earth Science

Earth has many different plants and animals. Earth also has many different places for plants and animals to live. Some plants and animals live in deserts like the one in this picture. The desert is hot and dry. Winds blow the sand. Sometimes, rain falls and floods the desert floor. The wind and rain carve rocks into interesting shapes. The desert, like other places on Earth, is always changing.

# CHAPTER 4

# The Living Earth

Plants and animals live together in ecosystems. In an ecosystem, every plant and animal is important. In the picture, the berry provides food for the bird. Inside the berry is a seed. First, the bird eats the berry. Then, the bird will drop the seed. The seed may grow into a new plant that will feed other birds. In this chapter you will learn more about how plants and animals live together in an ecosystem.

## What is it?

- It is a living part of an ecosystem.
- It uses other living things for food.
- It eats plants and animals.

# LESSON 1

# What Is an Ecosystem?

Every living thing on Earth is a part of an **ecosystem**. An ecosystem is a community of plants and animals in an area. One example of an ecosystem is a forest. Another example of an ecosystem is a stream. There are millions of ecosystems on Earth.

Every ecosystem has things that are **nonliving**, or not alive. Two nonliving things in a forest ecosystem are soil and air. Two nonliving things in a stream ecosystem are rocks and water. Other nonliving things in ecosystems are rain and sunlight. Nonliving things are important to the living plants and animals in the ecosystem.

Every ecosystem has living things in it. For example, a forest ecosystem can have bears, foxes, rabbits, and many other animals. The trees and other plants are also part of a forest ecosystem. A stream ecosystem can have fish, frogs, insects, and many other animals. The plants that grow in the stream are also part of the stream ecosystem.

An ecosystem can be large or small. An ocean is a very large ecosystem. It is made up of the living animals and plants and the nonliving water. An old log on the ground is a very small ecosystem. It is made up of the nonliving log and the living things, such as insects, that make the log their home.

Earth has many different ecosystems. A forest ecosystem is different from a desert ecosystem. A mountain ecosystem is different from a lake ecosystem. But all ecosystems are the same in one important way. Every ecosystem gives the living things in it what they need to live. Ecosystems are the homes for all living things on Earth.

**A Stream Ecosystem**

## A.

**Write True if the sentence is true. Write False if the sentence is false.**

_____ 1. An ecosystem is a community of plants and animals in an area.

_____ 2. Every ecosystem includes both living and nonliving things.

_____ 3. All ecosystems are equal in size.

_____ 4. There are many different kinds of ecosystems.

## B.

**Look at the picture of the forest ecosystem. Write the living and nonliving things shown in the picture.**

Living Things in a Forest Ecosystem

1. _____
2. _____
3. _____
4. _____

Nonliving Things in a Forest Ecosystem

1. _____
2. _____
3. _____
4. _____

## C.

**Write one or more sentences to answer the questions.**

Could a robin from a forest ecosystem live in a desert ecosystem? Why or why not?

_____
_____
_____
_____

# LESSON 2
## What Lives in an Ecosystem?

Every ecosystem on Earth has movement in it. Think about a forest ecosystem. A tree grows. A mouse runs across the forest floor. An eagle soars through the sky. All of this movement means that there is energy in the ecosystem. Living things get their energy in different ways.

Plants use sunlight to make their own food. They use this food to get energy to live and grow. Because they make food, they are called **producers**. Producers are the living things in an ecosystem that make food.

Unlike plants, animals in an ecosystem cannot make their own food. They have to eat other living things to get their energy. **Consumers** are living things in an ecosystem that eat other living things for food. There are three kinds of consumers. Consumers that eat only plants are called **herbivores**. Consumers that eat only animals are called **carnivores**. Consumers that eat both plants and animals are called **omnivores**.

There are also **decomposers** in an ecosystem. Decomposers are tiny living things that get their energy by eating dead plants and animals.

Producers, consumers, and decomposers all work together in an ecosystem. A plant gets energy by making food. A mouse gets energy by eating the plant. An eagle gets energy by eating the mouse. A decomposer gets energy by eating the eagle after it dies. This movement of energy as food through an ecosystem is called the **food chain**. The food chain shows that all of the living things in an ecosystem need one another.

The plant is a producer in a forest ecosystem. The mouse and the eagle are consumers.

## A. Write the word or words that best complete each sentence.

consumers        decomposers        food chain        producers

1. Living things in an ecosystem that make their own food are called _____.

2. Living things in an ecosystem that eat other living things are called _____.

3. Living things in an ecosystem that eat dead plants and animals are called _____.

4. The movement of energy as food through an ecosystem is called the _____.

## B. Look at the picture of the forest ecosystem. Use it to complete each list.

Producers in a Forest Ecosystem

1. _____
2. _____
3. _____

Consumers in a Forest Ecosystem

1. _____
2. _____
3. _____

## C. Look at the picture of the ecosystem above. Use it to answer the question.

The bird is a carnivore that eats animals to live. But it needs plants to live, too. How do you explain this?

_____
_____

# LESSON 3

# How Do Living Things Compete?

When you play a game, you **compete**, or try to win. Living things in an ecosystem compete, too. Each living thing competes to win what it needs to live. Competing with other living things is called **competition**. There is competition in every ecosystem on Earth.

Plants compete with other plants. For example, plants need water to live and grow. They compete with one another to win the water. Some plant roots grow down under the ground where there is water. Other plants try to win water by growing big leaves that catch rain. Plants also compete for other things they need, such as sunlight.

Animals in an ecosystem compete, too. They compete for food. For example, a fox needs to eat small animals, like mice, to live. Other foxes may try to eat the same mice. So to win, a fox has to be better at catching mice than other foxes. An owl might also want to eat the mice. The foxes might win by catching mice that an owl can't catch. Every animal does its best to win the food it needs to stay alive.

Besides food, animals compete for other things. They compete for water. They compete for the best places to live. They compete to see who will be the leader of their group.

Some animals sleep during the day and come out at night. In this way, they don't have to compete as much with daytime animals. This gives them a better chance of winning. It's another way living things compete in an ecosystem.

The foxes and owl compete for the mouse.

**A.** Write **True** if the sentence is true. Write **False** if the sentence is false.

_____ 1. Living things in an ecosystem compete.

_____ 2. Plants compete with other plants for water.

_____ 3. Foxes and owls work together to catch food.

_____ 4. Some animals come out at night so that they don't have to compete with daytime animals.

**B.** Write a sentence to answer each question.

1. What are two things plants compete for in an ecosystem?
   _____
   _____

2. What are two things animals compete for in an ecosystem?
   _____
   _____

**C.** Look at the picture. Then write a sentence to answer each question.

1. What example of competition does the picture show?
   _____
   _____
   _____

2. How will one animal win the competition?
   _____
   _____
   _____

LESSON

# How Do Ecosystems Change?

Ecosystems are always changing. It is easy to see some of these changes. Think about a forest ecosystem. You can see deer run and leaves fall from the trees. You can see water flow and birds fly. All of these things are changes in a forest ecosystem.

Ecosystems also change in much slower ways. Very important changes often happen slowly. For example, wind might blow new seeds into a desert ecosystem. Over time, the seeds may grow. Then, there is a new kind of plant in the desert ecosystem. Over many years, the new kind of plant may spread all over the desert. It would be a slow, but important, change in the desert ecosystem.

Other important changes in an ecosystem happen quickly. A forest fire can burn much of a forest. Or a stream flowing through the forest might flood. Many plants and animals would be killed. In just a few days, there is a very important change in the forest ecosystem.

So ecosystems change both slowly and quickly. Either way, changes in an ecosystem affect the living things in it. Some plants and animals live through the change. Others die. Sometimes, all of one kind of plant or animal are killed by a change in the ecosystem. That plant or animal is then called **extinct**. An animal or a plant is extinct when there are none of its kind left on Earth.

Most changes in ecosystems do not cause living things to become extinct. Most changes are much smaller. They are just part of life in an ecosystem, where things are always changing.

This stream has flooded. The flood will change the forest ecosystem.

**A.** Write **True** if the sentence is true. Write **False** if the sentence is false.

_____ 1. Ecosystems are always changing.

_____ 2. Ecosystems change both slowly and quickly.

_____ 3. Plants and animals always live through changes in an ecosystem.

_____ 4. A living thing is extinct when there are only a few of its kind left on Earth.

_____ 5. Most changes in ecosystems cause living things to become extinct.

**B.** Read each sentence. Write **Slow** if the sentence tells about a slow change to an ecosystem. Write **Fast** if the sentence tells about a fast change to an ecosystem.

_____ 1. A fox eats a rabbit.

_____ 2. A forest fire happens.

_____ 3. A stream floods in the forest.

_____ 4. A new type of seed begins to grow.

_____ 5. A baby wolf grows up.

_____ 6. A snake eats a mouse.

**C.** Write one or more sentences to answer the question.

How might an erupting volcano make a kind of plant extinct?

_____
_____
_____
_____
_____
_____

# LESSON 5

## How Do People Change Ecosystems?

Ecosystems change by themselves. Plants and animals are born, grow, and die. Streams flow. It rains a lot, and then the rain stops. All of these changes are natural parts of ecosystems.

But some of the biggest changes in ecosystems are made by people. Think about your community. There may have been a forest ecosystem where buildings now stand. There may have been fields with tall grass or a desert with cactus plants. People changed the ecosystem to make room for buildings. In doing so, they may have destroyed the ecosystem.

Of course, people don't always destroy ecosystems. They can change ecosystems without destroying them. For example, if people build a road through a forest, the forest ecosystem is changed. Trees are cut down to make room for the road. The noise from cars driving on the road may scare some animals. The forest ecosystem is different, but not destroyed.

People have also changed ecosystems by adding **pollution**. Pollution is harmful waste that can hurt an ecosystem. Air pollution from cars and factories hurts plants and animals. Land pollution, such as trash and litter, also hurts living things. Water pollution kills many living things in lakes, rivers, streams, and oceans.

Not all of the changes people make to ecosystems are harmful. Many people help ecosystems, for example, by planting new trees. But sadly, people have hurt ecosystems more than they have helped them.

People are changing this forest ecosystem to make room for a road.

Pollution can hurt animals.

**A.** Write the missing word or words in each sentence.

1. Some of the biggest _____ in an ecosystem are made by people.
   (plants, animals, changes)

2. If people build a road through a forest, the noise from cars on the road may _____ some animals.
   (scare, help, feed)

3. Harmful waste that can hurt an ecosystem is called _____.
   (community, building, pollution)

4. Air pollution from factories and _____ has hurt living things.
   (plants, cars, rivers)

5. One way to help an ecosystem is to _____ new trees.
   (pollute, cut down, plant)

**B.** List three ways that people have changed ecosystems.

1. _____
2. _____
3. _____

**C.** Write one or more sentences to answer the question.

Imagine that water pollution from a new factory kills all the small fish in a lake. What might this do to the rest of the lake ecosystem?

_____
_____
_____
_____

67

LESSON

# 6. How Can People Protect Ecosystems?

People have changed ecosystems all over Earth. In many places, entire ecosystems have been destroyed to make room for buildings. In many other places, pollution has damaged ecosystems.

But people have also worked hard to protect ecosystems. One way people protect ecosystems is by making **nature preserves**. Nature preserves are special parks where plants and animals live. These are not the kinds of parks with slides and swings. In nature preserves, nature is left alone. The ecosystems in nature preserves are protected from some of the changes people cause.

You can also help protect ecosystems. How? Since pollution hurts ecosystems, you can help by trying not to pollute. The best way to do this is by following "the three R's." The three R's stand for **reduce**, **reuse**, and **recycle**.

To **reduce** means to use less of things that can cause pollution. For example, instead of using paper napkins, you can use cloth napkins that can be washed. This will lower the number of paper napkins that people throw away.

To **reuse** means to use things over and over again instead of throwing them away. For example, you can reuse a shopping bag many times. You can take it back to the store instead of throwing it away.

To **recycle** means to use old things to make new things. Old metal cans are melted down and used to make new metal cans. Old newspapers are used to make new paper.

Nature preserves are an important way to protect ecosystems.

### A. Write a sentence to answer each question.

1. What is a nature preserve?

   _____
   _____

2. Why do people make nature preserves?

   _____
   _____

3. What do "the three R's" stand for?

   _____
   _____

4. How does following "the three R's" help protect ecosystems?

   _____
   _____

### B. Read each statement. Write reduce, reuse, or recycle to tell what the statement describes.

_____ 1. Students work together to collect aluminum cans in the community.

_____ 2. A student keeps her rock collection in an old shoe box.

_____ 3. A student carries his lunch in a lunch box instead of paper bags.

### C. Write one or more sentences to answer the question.

Why do you think people like to visit nature preserves and see ecosystems that are not polluted?

_____
_____

# CHAPTER 4

# Watch an Ecosystem in Action

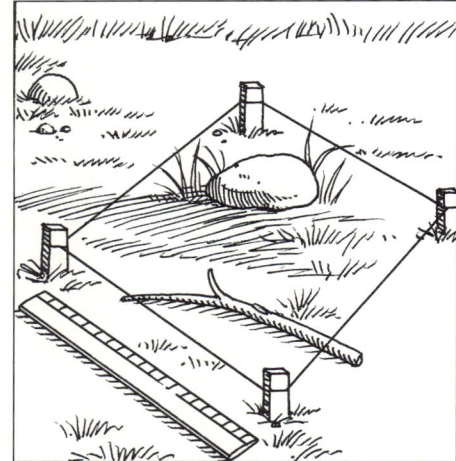

**You need:**

- meterstick
- 4 wooden sticks
- string
- scissors
- hand lens
- paper and pencil

**In this activity you will observe an ecosystem.**

Follow these steps:

1. Use a meterstick to mark off a one-meter square on the ground. Push the wooden sticks into the ground to make the corners of the square. Loop the string around the sticks and tie it to make the sides of the square.

2. Make a list of all the living and nonliving things inside the square. Watch for any activity inside the square for about 15 minutes. Record what you see.

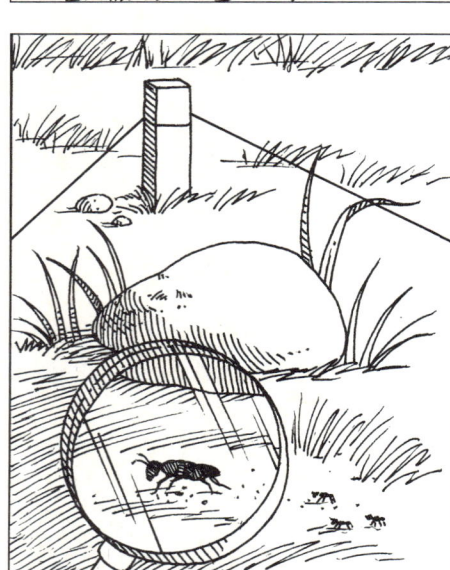

**Write answers to these questions.**

1. What living and nonliving things did you find inside the square?

   _____
   _____

2. What activity did you see?

   _____
   _____

3. What does one living thing you saw need to stay alive?

   _____
   _____

# TEST CHAPTER 4

**Darken the circle next to the correct answer.**

1. Every living thing on Earth is part of
   - Ⓐ a desert.
   - Ⓑ an ocean.
   - Ⓒ an ecosystem.
   - Ⓓ a forest.

2. How many ecosystems are there on Earth?
   - Ⓐ one
   - Ⓑ two
   - Ⓒ hundreds
   - Ⓓ millions

3. Living things that use energy from sunlight to make their own food are called
   - Ⓐ producers.
   - Ⓑ consumers.
   - Ⓒ decomposers.
   - Ⓓ herbivores.

4. What is the movement of energy as food through an ecosystem called?
   - Ⓐ competition
   - Ⓑ herbivore
   - Ⓒ food chain
   - Ⓓ nature preserve

5. Plants in an ecosystem compete for
   - Ⓐ water and sunlight.
   - Ⓑ food and nests.
   - Ⓒ herbivores.
   - Ⓓ carnivores.

6. If an animal is extinct, how many are left on Earth?
   - Ⓐ none
   - Ⓑ one
   - Ⓒ a few
   - Ⓓ hundreds

7. Harmful waste that can hurt an ecosystem is called
   - Ⓐ a decomposer.
   - Ⓑ energy.
   - Ⓒ the food chain.
   - Ⓓ pollution.

8. A special place where nature is protected is called
   - Ⓐ an herbivore.
   - Ⓑ an ecosystem.
   - Ⓒ a nature preserve.
   - Ⓓ a forest.

9. To use washable plates instead of paper plates is to
   - Ⓐ reduce.
   - Ⓑ reuse.
   - Ⓒ return.
   - Ⓓ recycle.

10. To use a shopping bag over and over again is to
    - Ⓐ reduce.
    - Ⓑ reuse.
    - Ⓒ return.
    - Ⓓ recycle.

CHAPTER 5

# Earth's Surface

What happens if you climb a mountain? At first, you may pass through forests. Then the air gets colder, and there aren't as many trees. Soon the ground is covered with snow, and all the trees are gone. Such changes don't happen if you climb a hill. Why not? In this chapter you will learn more about the different shapes of land on Earth and how they are formed.

What is it?

- It changes the land slowly.
- It wears away even tall mountains.
- Rain and wind can cause it.

# LESSON 1

# What Are Landforms?

What if you could walk across a different place in the world every day? If you did, the land in each place might have a different shape. Land can rise up and drop down in many ways. One day you might walk up a steep slope. Another day you might walk down a gentle hill. And one day, the ground you are walking on might be very flat for miles and miles. You would be walking across different **landforms**. A landform is a shape on Earth's surface.

A **mountain** is the highest landform. There aren't many flat places on a mountain. Sometimes even the top is not flat. If you walk on a mountain, you either have to climb up or go down. Some mountains are so high that they are almost impossible to climb. Trees grow on the sides of many mountains. But often the tops of high mountains are too cold and windy for trees to live. These mountains are often covered in snow.

A **hill** rises above the land around it, but it is not as high as a mountain. Hills are more rounded than mountains, and have few steep slopes.

A landform called a **plateau** can rise as high as a mountain. A plateau has very steep sides that rise above the surrrounding land. However, plateaus are flat on top.

The lowest type of landform is called a **plain**. A plain is mostly flat or gently rolling. It does not rise above the surrounding land. Plains can spread for miles and miles. They can be covered with grass. Often large groups of animals, such as buffalo, live on plains and eat the grass there.

## Types of Landforms

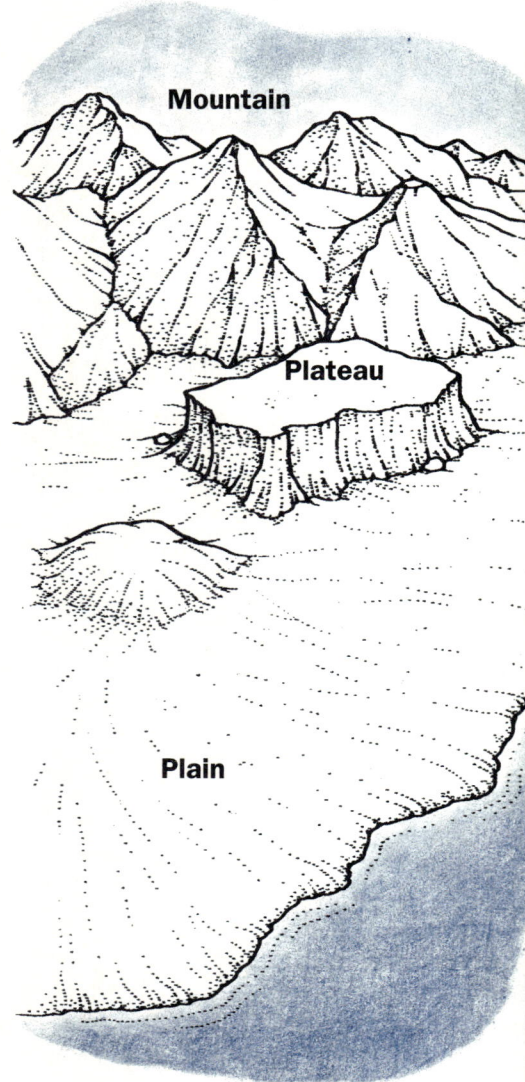

74

**A.** Draw a line to match the name of the landform with the sentence that describes it.

1. plain — This landform is also high, but it is very flat.
2. mountain — This landform usually has a rounded shape.
3. plateau — This is the highest landform with few flat places.
4. hill — This is a low, flat, or rolling landform that can be covered with grass.

**B.** Write the word that best completes each sentence.

buffalo    landform    mountain    plain    trees

1. A shape on Earth's surface is called a _____.
2. There are few flat places on a _____.
3. The tops of some mountains can be too cold and windy for _____ to live.
4. A plateau is flat, but it is higher than a _____.
5. Animals that eat grass, such as _____, might live on plains.

**C.** Write one or more sentences to answer the questions.

Pretend you are walking. You climb up a steep slope for a long way. When you reach the top, you go down another long, steep slope. There are no flat places. What kind of landform are you on? How do you know?

_____
_____
_____

# LESSON 2

## How Do Landforms Change Slowly?

Landforms are always changing. Most landforms change so slowly that you may never notice what is happening.

Wind, rain, ice, and snow break and wear away even the tallest mountain. Each drop of rain changes a landform in a small way. The breaking and wearing away of landforms is called **weathering**.

Strong winds and flowing water carry away the broken pieces of landforms. This is called **erosion**. Together, erosion and weathering change the shapes of landforms.

Erosion can move large pieces of rock as well as tiny grains of sand. Erosion carries some pieces of rock into streams and rivers. Imagine a big rock resting on the bottom of a stream. Erosion carries more rocks into the stream all the time. These rocks hit the large rock. They break small pieces off the large rock. The small pieces are washed away. The sand carried by the stream also wears away the big rock. Over many years, the rock is carved into a new shape. It may even be worn away completely.

Wind can also carry soil and broken pieces of rock. When the wind blows against the side of a mountain, the soil and rock pieces that it carries slowly carve the mountain away. The mountain is like the rock in the stream. In time, it is changed by weathering and erosion. You can't see each change. But after many years, you can see the big changes in landforms.

Wind, snow, and ice wear away even the tallest mountains.

Winds and flowing water change the shapes of mountains.

## A. Write True if the sentence is true. Write False if the sentence is false.

_____ 1. Most landforms change shape quickly.

_____ 2. Weathering is the breaking and wearing away of landforms.

_____ 3. Erosion keeps rocks and sand from moving.

_____ 4. Water and wind can carry tiny pieces of rock.

_____ 5. Erosion only happens to very small rocks.

## B. Write the word or words that best complete each sentence.

| | | |
|---|---|---|
| **landform** | **very slowly** | **wind** |
| **pieces of rock** | **weathering** | |

1. The way the wind, rain, ice, and snow break and wear away landforms is called _____.

2. Erosion can carry away broken pieces of a _____.

3. Erosion is caused by water and _____.

4. Wind can carry _____ that can carve away a mountain.

5. Weathering and erosion change landforms _____.

## C. Write one or more sentences to answer the question.

Imagine that a big rock falls into a stream. At first, the side of this rock is very rough and bumpy, with sharp edges. But many years later, the side of the rock is smooth. How did this happen?

_____

_____

## LESSON 3

# How Do Landforms Change Quickly?

Imagine that you are on a fishing boat on the ocean. You notice a strange smell in the air. Your boat begins to rock. You see a cloud of fiery pieces of rock. The cloud grows taller and taller. In only a few hours, a new island is born.

Sometimes, changes on Earth happen quickly. Earth is made of **layers**. The outside layer, called the **crust**, is made of rocks. Deep inside Earth, it is very hot. The heat melts the rocks in the bottom of the crust. Melted rock moves up and spills through cracks in the crust. Each crack in the crust where hot, melted rock spills out on the surface is a **volcano**. The melted rock cools and hardens. It makes a new landform.

**Earthquakes** can also change landforms quickly. Earth's crust is made of large pieces called **plates**. These plates move. Sometimes, the plates push against each other. Sometimes, they rub past each other. And sometimes, they pull away from each other. When plates push, rub, or pull with great force, waves of energy move through the ground. We feel Earth shake.

When Earth shakes, the land can change quickly. Deep cracks appear suddenly in the ground. Loose rocks and soil tumble down steep mountains. This is called a **landslide**. Huge ocean waves may flood the land. Sometimes, volcanoes **erupt**, or explode. Even rivers may change the direction in which they flow.

Volcanoes and earthquakes have the power to change landforms in a short time. But most changes to Earth's landforms are slow and steady.

**How a Volcano Forms**

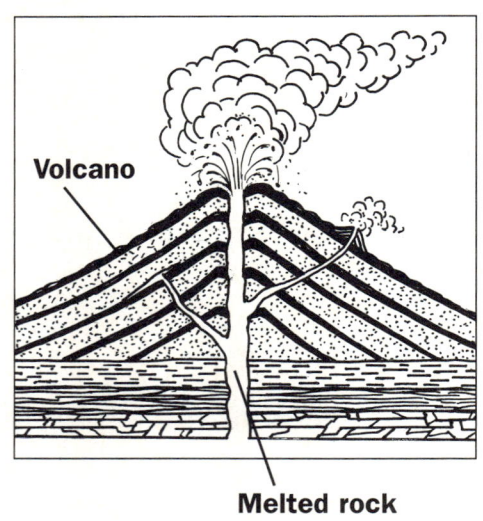

## A. Choose the word or words that best complete each sentence.

1. Volcanoes change landforms _____.
   (slowly, quickly, very little)

2. The outside layer of Earth is called the _____.
   (rock, crust, plate)

3. Deep inside Earth, the temperature is _____.
   (hot, cold, low)

## B. Write the word that best completes each sentence.

| earthquake | landform | move | volcano |

1. When melted rock from inside Earth spills through a crack onto the surface, a _____ forms.

2. The melted rock may make a new _____.

3. Earthquakes may happen when the plates that make up Earth's crust _____.

4. The land shakes and can crack during an _____.

## C. Write one or more sentences to answer the question.

Imagine that you live near mountains. You are eating dinner when suddenly, the dishes begin to move around on the table. You feel the floor moving. You hear a roar. When things are quiet, you run to look out the window. A pile of rocks has appeared in your neighbors' yard. What do you think has happened?

_____

_____

_____

# LESSON 4

# How Do Rocks Form and Change?

Rocks form in different ways. One kind of rock forms when melted rock from inside Earth cools. This kind of rock is called **igneous** rock. In places where there are many volcanoes, igneous rock covers much of the ground.

New rock also forms when small pieces of other rocks or parts of dead plants or animals are pressed together very hard. This kind of rock is called **sedimentary** rock.

Sedimentary rock can form under water. The moving water of a river carries bits of rock and other things. When the river reaches the ocean, the things it was carrying fall to the ocean bottom. Seashells also fall to the bottom. Over time, more and more rock and other bits are added. After these things are pressed together for millions of years, they form sedimentary rock. If you look at a piece of sedimentary rock, you might see pebbles, sand, or even seashells in it.

Earthquakes can force rocks deep into Earth, where they are squeezed hard. This changes rock. So does the heat inside Earth. When rock is changed this way, it is called **metamorphic** rock.

Rocks can change from one kind to another in other ways. Sedimentary rock may fall into a crack in Earth's surface during an earthquake. Inside Earth, the rock melts. If the melted rock comes up through a volcano and cools, it becomes igneous rock. Pieces of the igneous rock may fall into a stream where they are carried away by erosion. When these pieces reach the ocean, they fall to the ocean floor. There these pieces can form new sedimentary rock.

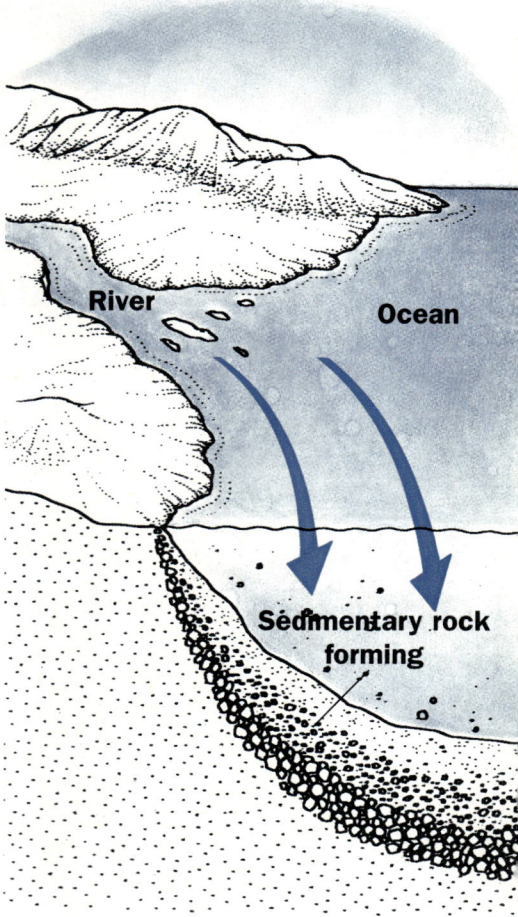

Sedimentary rock can be formed when sand, shells, and pieces of rock fall to the bottom of the ocean and are pressed together.

**A.** Write in the word that best completes each sentence.

1. Melted rock cools to form _____ rock.
   (igneous, sedimentary, metamorphic)

2. Pieces that make up sedimentary rock are _____ together.
   (stirred, pressed, melted)

3. Rock can be forced deep into Earth by _____.
   (earthquakes, erosion, weathering)

4. Inside of Earth, squeezing and heat form _____ rock.
   (igneous, sedimentary, metamorphic)

5. Tiny rock pieces carried away by water can form new _____ rock.
   (igneous, sedimentary, metamorphic)

**B.** Write **True** if the sentence is true. Write **False** if the sentence is false.

_____ 1. Igneous rock is formed from seashells.

_____ 2. Sedimentary rock is formed only on mountaintops.

_____ 3. Small pieces of rock can be pressed into sedimentary rock.

_____ 4. Metamorphic rock has been changed inside Earth.

_____ 5. Rocks never change from one kind to another.

**C.** Write one or more sentences to answer the questions.

You are digging a garden in your yard. You find rocks with bits of seashells in them. What kind of rock did you find? How do you think it got into your garden soil?

_____

_____

_____

## LESSON 5

# What Is the Ocean Like?

Water covers about three-quarters of our planet. Many kinds of plants and animals live in the ocean. Plants need light, so they live near the top of the ocean. But animals can live at the bottom of the ocean.

The bottom of the ocean is known as the **ocean floor**. The ocean floor isn't all flat. Like land, it has mountains and valleys. The longest mountain chain on Earth runs along the bottom of the ocean.

The part of the ocean floor closest to land is the **continental shelf**. On the continental shelf, the water is not as deep as it is in other parts of the ocean. Most ocean animals live there. It is the home of corals and small, colorful fish.

If you travel on a boat far away from the shore, you will come to the **open ocean**. Here, the water is much deeper. Fish of all shapes and sizes live in the open ocean. Other animals, such as turtles and whales, also live in the open ocean.

The deepest part of the ocean is called the **abyss**. The abyss is very dark. It is so deep that the light of the sun does not reach it. Very few animals live there. No plants live in the abyss.

**Ocean currents** are rivers of water that flow through the ocean around them. Ocean currents bring warm water to colder parts of the ocean. One current, the Gulf Stream, makes weather warmer in the northern countries of Britain and Norway. Ocean currents also bring special materials to the surface. Ocean plants use this material to stay healthy. These plants are food for many ocean animals.

### Parts of the Ocean

The arrows show how ocean currents move through the ocean.

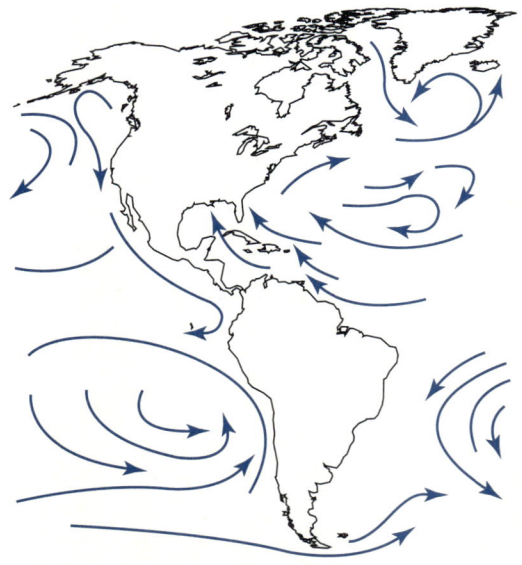

**A.** Write the missing word or words in each sentence.

1. Water covers about _____ of Earth.
   (one-quarter, one-half, three-quarters)

2. The deepest part of the ocean is the _____.
   (continental shelf, abyss, Gulf Stream)

3. Rivers that move through the ocean are called _____.
   (the open ocean, the abyss, ocean currents)

**B.** Write <u>True</u> if the sentence is true. Write <u>False</u> if the sentence is false.

_____ 1. Plants do not live deep below the ocean's surface.

_____ 2. The ocean floor is completely flat.

_____ 3. Ocean currents help keep ocean plants and animals healthy.

**C.** Draw a line to complete each sentence.

1. Ocean currents             are rivers of moving ocean water.

2. The abyss                  is the part of the ocean floor closest to land.

3. The ocean floor            is the deepest part of the ocean.

4. The continental shelf      is the bottom of the ocean.

**D.** Write one or more sentences to answer the question.

Why do you think that more animals live near the surface of the ocean than in the deeper parts?

_____

_____

_____

_____

# LESSON 6
## How Do People Affect the Ocean?

The ocean is important to people in many ways. Much of our food comes from the ocean. Many kinds of fish are caught to feed hungry people. Other ocean animals, such as clams and shrimp, are also used for food. Even seaweed is used for food.

Another way the ocean is important is that **ships** can travel on it. Ships bring food, clothing, and other things to different parts of the world.

The ocean is also important to us because there is **oil** under the ocean floor. People use oil to run factories and cars and to heat their homes. Large machines dig deep under the ocean floor to find oil. Then, the oil is carried in huge ships called **tankers**. Tankers take the oil all over the world.

Sometimes, a tanker carrying oil crashes or sinks. When this happens, the oil that the tanker carries leaks out into the ocean. This is called an **oil spill**. The oil poisons ocean plants and animals. They die, and the animals that eat them have no food. Oil from a spill may cover the feathers of sea birds and keep them from flying.

Even though the ocean is very important, sometimes we don't take good care of it. People put all kinds of pollution into the ocean. Sometimes we throw our garbage into the ocean or into waters that flow into the ocean. This garbage can hurt or kill ocean plants and animals. For example, a sea turtle can choke on a sandwich bag, or a sea bird can become tangled in string and drown.

The ocean is home to many plants and animals. It also feeds millions of people. People need to keep the ocean clean and safe for living things.

## How People Use the Ocean

**Food**

**Ships**

**Oil**

## A. Write the word or words that best complete each sentence.

clean    oil spill    tanker    food    pollution

1. Fish, clams, and seaweed are kinds of _____ from the ocean.

2. A large ship that carries oil is called a _____.

3. Oil that leaks from a ship into the ocean is an _____.

4. People harm ocean life when they put _____ into the ocean.

5. It is important to keep the ocean _____.

## B. Underline the correct word or words in each sentence.

1. The ocean has oil (under the ocean floor, inside waves) that people use.

2. Ships are important because they bring (pollution, food) and other things people need.

3. When people put (garbage, food) into the ocean, plants and animals can become sick or die.

## C. Write one or more sentences to answer the question.

Some people call the ocean a huge highway. How is the ocean like a highway?

_____
_____
_____
_____

# CHAPTER 5

# Observe Erosion

**You need:**

- large pan
- sand
- water
- straw

**In this activity you will see how erosion works.**

Follow these steps:

1. Put sand into the pan. Add water to make the sand wet. Shape the wet sand into landforms, such as mountains, plains, and plateaus. Put some dry sand on top of the landforms.

2. Pour water on the landforms. Pour a little bit of water slowly. Then, pour a lot of water quickly. Watch what happens.

3. Use the straw to blow against the landforms to model wind. Blow at different speeds and from different directions. Watch what happens.

**Write answers to these questions.**

1. What happened when water was added to the different landforms?

2. How did the wind affect the landforms?

3. Did the wind act in the same way on the wet sand and on the dry sand? Explain.

# TEST  CHAPTER 5

**Darken the circle next to the correct answer.**

1. The different shapes of land on Earth are called
   - Ⓐ mountains.
   - Ⓑ earthquakes.
   - Ⓒ ground.
   - Ⓓ landforms.

2. A flat landform that can be as high as a mountain is called a
   - Ⓐ plain.
   - Ⓑ plateau.
   - Ⓒ hill.
   - Ⓓ cliff.

3. Which of these can change landforms slowly?
   - Ⓐ volcanoes
   - Ⓑ earthquakes
   - Ⓒ weathering
   - Ⓓ landslides

4. What does wind or water carry that causes erosion?
   - Ⓐ tiny pieces of rock
   - Ⓑ fish and plants
   - Ⓒ smoke
   - Ⓓ dead leaves

5. The outside layer of Earth is called the
   - Ⓐ rock layer.
   - Ⓑ melted rock.
   - Ⓒ crust.
   - Ⓓ plate.

6. What kind of rock forms when melted rock cools?
   - Ⓐ metamorphic rock
   - Ⓑ sedimentary rock
   - Ⓒ changed rock
   - Ⓓ igneous rock

7. Sedimentary rock forms when pieces of rocks, plants, or animals
   - Ⓐ float in water.
   - Ⓑ are pressed together.
   - Ⓒ are melted.
   - Ⓓ fall into a deep crack.

8. Most ocean animals live in the waters
   - Ⓐ near the ocean floor.
   - Ⓑ of the abyss.
   - Ⓒ of the continental shelf.
   - Ⓓ of the open ocean.

9. The deepest part of the ocean is known as the
   - Ⓐ abyss.
   - Ⓑ continental shelf.
   - Ⓒ ocean current.
   - Ⓓ open ocean.

10. What do people need to do to take care of the ocean?
    - Ⓐ wash the beach often
    - Ⓑ throw things into it
    - Ⓒ boil ocean water
    - Ⓓ keep it clean for living things

88

# CHAPTER 6

# Our Solar System

Earth is one of the nine planets that make our solar system. The planets orbit the sun, but this picture doesn't show a planet. The moon orbits Earth, but this picture doesn't show the moon either. Other kinds of objects, such as meteors, also orbit the sun. But only a comet has a tail like the one in the picture. In this chapter you will learn all about the many objects in our solar system.

What is it?

- It circles the sun.
- It has rocky landforms.
- It has a red surface.

# LESSON 1

## What Tools Do Astronomers Use?

Have you ever looked at the stars in the night sky? Then you have done the same thing that **astronomers** do. Astronomers are scientists who study stars and other objects in space.

Like you, the first astronomers used their eyes to study the night sky. For thousands of years, people looked at the stars and the moon. They wondered about them and drew maps of the night sky.

Then, about four hundred years ago, the **optical telescope** was invented. An optical telescope is a tool that collects light waves. It makes objects that are far away look closer. Optical telescopes let people see things in space more clearly. They also let people see things in space that they were not able to see using only their eyes. Today, optical telescopes are more powerful than ever. Astronomers use them to discover new things in space.

Astronomers also use other kinds of telescopes. For example, things in space give off radio waves. Radio waves are a kind of energy that you can't see with your eyes. A **radio telescope** collects radio waves. Astronomers use computers to study these radio waves and learn about objects in space.

Besides telescopes, another important tool astronomers use is a **space probe**. A space probe is a spacecraft sent into space to explore. Some space probes land on other planets. Space probes send pictures and other information back to astronomers on Earth. Like telescopes, space probes have shown astronomers a lot more than they could see with just their eyes.

**Radio Telescope**

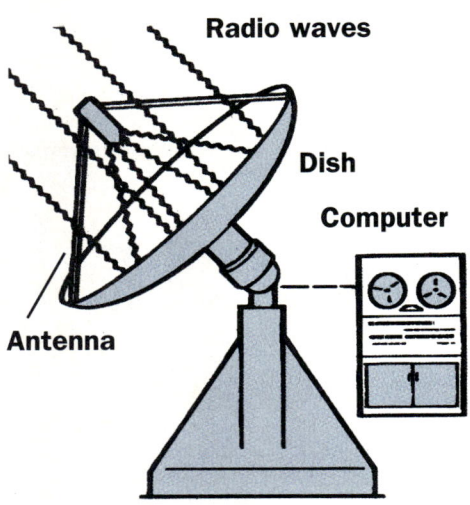

This photo shows the Sojourner rover of the Mars Pathfinder mission exploring the surface of Mars.

**A.** Put a ✔ next to the tools that astronomers use.

_____ 1. optical telescope

_____ 2. stars

_____ 3. radio telescope

_____ 4. moon

_____ 5. space probe

**B.** Write <u>True</u> if the sentence is true. Write <u>False</u> if the sentence is false.

_____ 1. Scientists who study stars and other objects in space are called astronomers.

_____ 2. Astronomers use optical telescopes to study radio waves.

_____ 3. The radio telescope was invented about four hundred years ago.

_____ 4. Space probes send pictures and other information back to astronomers on Earth.

**C.** Write one or more sentences to answer the question.

What is the difference between an optical telescope and a radio telescope?

_____
_____
_____

**D.** Write one or more sentences to answer the question.

Astronomers have sent space probes to objects close in space, but not to those very far away. Why do you think this is so?

_____
_____
_____

# LESSON 2: What Is Our Solar System?

You live in your home. You live in your community. And you live on Earth. But did you know you also live in our **solar system**? Our solar system is the sun and everything that circles it.

The largest objects that **orbit**, or circle, the sun are called **planets**. Including Earth, there are nine planets in our solar system. You might have heard of some of the other planets in our solar system, such as Mars, Venus, or Saturn.

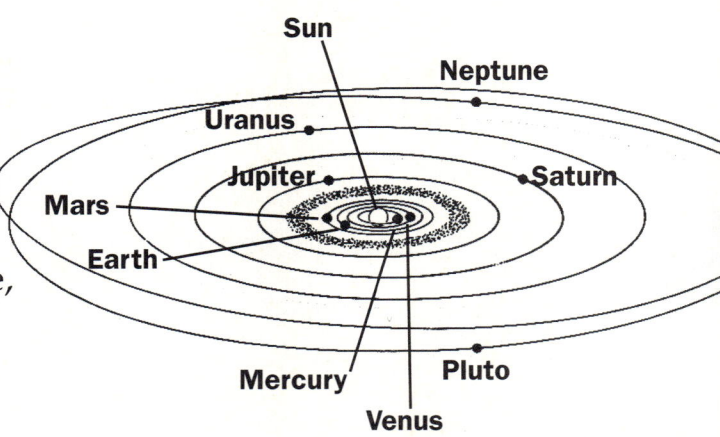

Our solar system includes the sun and the nine planets that circle around it.

The planets orbit the sun because of **gravity**. Gravity is the force that pulls objects toward each other. When you drop a pencil, gravity is what pulls it toward Earth. In the same way, gravity from the sun pulls the planets toward it. The planets don't fall into the sun because they are moving very fast and are far enough away from the sun. But they aren't fast enough to get away from the sun. So the planets continue circling the sun.

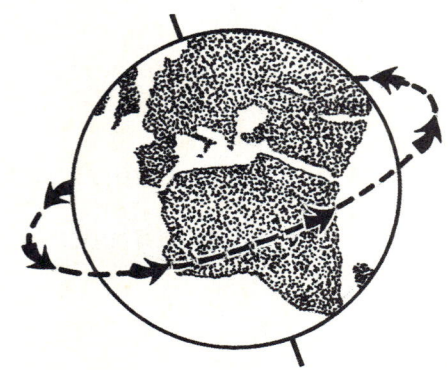

As Earth orbits the sun, it also rotates, or spins.

It takes Earth about 365 days to go around the sun. If this number sounds familiar, it's because this is the same number of days that are in a **year**. A year is the time that it takes Earth to make one complete circle around the sun.

As Earth circles the sun, it also spins, or **rotates**, just like a top. It takes about 24 hours for Earth to rotate once. This number might sound familiar, too. That's because it's the same number of hours in a **day**. A day is the time it takes Earth to rotate once. And every day is another day you live in our solar system!

**A.** Draw a line to connect each word to its definition.

1. solar system — large object that circles the sun
2. planet — force that pulls objects to each other
3. orbit — to spin like a top
4. gravity — sun and everything that circles it
5. year — time it takes Earth to circle the sun once
6. rotate — time it takes Earth to spin around once
7. day — to circle the sun or other object

**B.** Write the missing word or words in each sentence.

1. The solar system includes the planets that orbit _____.

   (the sun, the moon, Earth)

2. There are _____ planets in the solar system.

   (eight, nine, ten)

3. Every time Earth spins around once, one _____ goes by.

   (year, month, day)

4. Every time Earth orbits the sun, one _____ goes by.

   (year, month, day)

**C.** Write one or more sentences to answer the question.

About how many times does Earth rotate in one year?

_____
_____
_____
_____

93

# LESSON 3

## What Is the Moon?

On many nights, the brightest object we see in the sky is the **moon**. The moon is Earth's partner in space. It orbits, or goes around, Earth about once each month.

At night the moon can look bright. But the moon doesn't make its own light. It reflects, or gives back, light from the sun. When we see a bright moon, we see reflected sunlight.

The sun lights the moon in different ways at different times. Sometimes the moon looks like a bright circle. At other times the moon looks like a thick eyelash. These changes in the way the moon looks are called the **phases** of the moon. When the moon looks round, it is called a **full moon**. When the moon looks like an eyelash, it is called a **crescent moon**.

The moon is the only place beyond Earth that people have visited. In 1969 **astronauts** first landed on the moon. Astronauts are people who are specially trained to travel into and study space. Astronauts have brought back moon rocks and soil to study. They have also collected information about the moon using special tools.

The moon is much smaller than Earth. If Earth were the size of a basketball, the moon would be about the size of a tennis ball. There is no air or flowing water on the moon's surface. There are many landforms, such as mountains and valleys. The most common landforms on the moon are **craters**. Craters are holes in the ground. Most of the moon's craters were made by pieces of rock that fell from space.

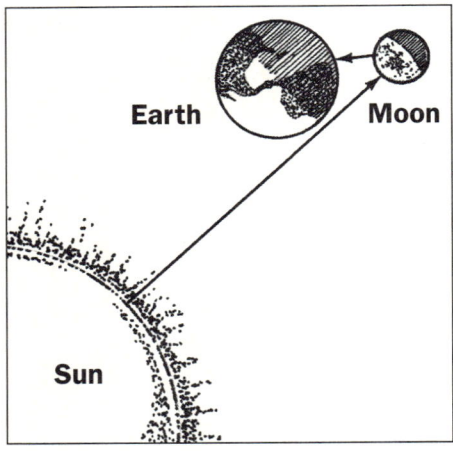

The moon looks bright because it reflects light from the sun toward Earth.

Astronauts visited the moon between 1969 and 1972.

## A. Write True if the sentence is true. Write False if the sentence is false.

_____ 1. Earth orbits the moon.

_____ 2. The moon reflects light from the sun.

_____ 3. The moon is bigger than Earth.

_____ 4. There are air and water on both Earth and the moon.

_____ 5. There are mountains and valleys on the moon's surface.

## B. Write the word that best completes each sentence.

| craters | crescent | full | month | phases |

1. It takes about one _____ for the moon to orbit Earth.

2. The different ways the moon looks at different times are called the _____ of the moon.

3. When the moon looks round, it is called a _____ moon.

4. When the moon looks like a thick eyelash, it is called a _____ moon.

5. The moon is covered with holes called _____ .

## C. Write one or more sentences to answer the question.

When rocks from space hit Earth, they can make a crater. But weathering and erosion can erase the crater. Craters on the moon can last millions of years. Why?

_____

_____

_____

95

# LESSON 4 What Are the Inner Planets?

Each planet in our solar system orbits the sun at a different distance. The four planets that orbit closest to the sun are called the **inner planets.** The inner planets are **Mercury**, **Venus**, **Earth**, and **Mars**.

Each inner planet is different. For example, Earth is the only planet with flowing water. But the planets are also the same in important ways. They all have rocky landforms, such as plains, mountains, and craters. They are surrounded by **atmospheres**, or layers of air. And each inner planet has iron, a metal, in its center.

The planet closest to the sun is **Mercury**. It is the smallest of the inner planets. Mercury's atmosphere is very thin. During the day the sun makes the surface very hot. At night the surface becomes very cold.

The second planet from the sun is **Venus**. Venus is Earth's closest neighbor. It is about the same size as Earth. The atmosphere on Venus has yellow-white clouds of acid. This keeps Venus even hotter than Mercury.

The third planet from the sun is **Earth**. Although its surface has landforms like the other inner planets, its atmosphere is very different. Earth is the only planet we know that has life.

The next planet beyond Earth is **Mars**. Mars is the last inner planet. Space probes have sent pictures of the planet's red surface. Mars has plains, sand dunes, craters, and volcanoes. It has ice caps around both its north and south poles. Mars has two moons that orbit it.

Mercury

Venus

Earth

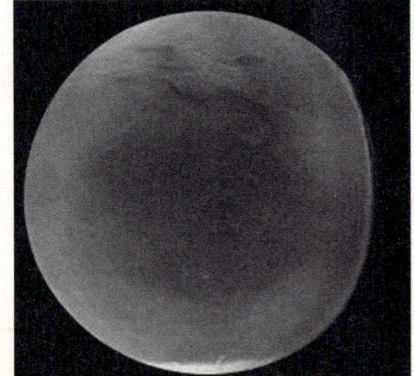
Mars

**A.** The inner planets are listed below. Write 1, 2, 3, and 4 to show the correct order of the inner planets from the sun.

_____ Earth

_____ Mercury

_____ Mars

_____ Venus

**B.** Underline the correct word in each sentence.

1. The four planets closest to the sun have rocky (landforms, gases, centers), such as plains and mountains.

2. The smallest of the inner planets is (Mercury, Venus, Earth).

3. Earth is about the same size as the planet (Mercury, Venus, Mars).

4. The planet Mars has two (atmospheres, volcanoes, moons) that orbit around it.

**C.** Write the name of the inner planet that each sentence describes.

_____ 1. This inner planet is closest to the sun.

_____ 2. This inner planet's atmosphere has yellowish clouds of acid.

_____ 3. This inner planet is the only one known to have life.

_____ 4. This inner planet has a red surface.

**D.** Write one or more sentences to answer the question.

All of the inner planets have atmospheres. But people can only breathe the air on Earth. Why do you think this is so?

_____

_____

_____

## LESSON 5

# What Are the Outer Planets?

Beyond Mars five more planets orbit the sun. These are the **outer planets**. They are **Jupiter, Saturn, Uranus, Neptune,** and **Pluto**.

Astronomers call most of the outer planets "giants," because they are very large. The surfaces and atmospheres of the giants are very different from the inner planets. The surfaces are not hard. Some of them have colorful clouds of gas.

**Jupiter** is the first of the outer planets. Jupiter is the largest planet in the solar system. More than one thousand Earths could fit inside Jupiter! Clouds and winds make Jupiter's atmosphere look red, yellow, brown, and white. One storm of winds, called the Great Red Spot, has been blowing for more than 300 years. Jupiter has rings around it as well as 16 moons.

**Saturn** is the next planet from the sun. It is almost as big as Jupiter. Large, beautiful rings made of ice circle the planet. Saturn has at least 18 moons. This is more than any other planet.

**Uranus** is the next giant planet. It looks blue-green in color to astronomers because of the gases in its thin atmosphere. Like Jupiter and Saturn, Uranus also has rings that circle it. But Uranus doesn't have nearly as many moons. Uranus has 15 moons.

The last giant planet is **Neptune**. It is very much like Uranus. Neptune looks blue. It has rings and 8 moons.

The last known planet in the solar system is **Pluto**. Pluto is the smallest planet. Its surface is hard and cold. Like Earth, Pluto has one moon.

Jupiter

Saturn

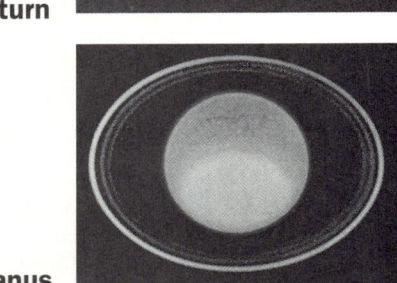
Uranus

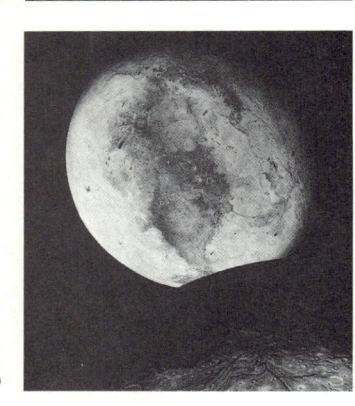
Pluto

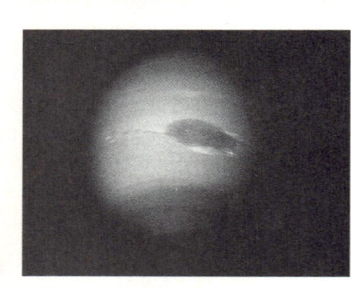
Neptune

**A.** The outer planets are listed below. Write 1, 2, 3, 4, and 5 to show the correct order of the outer planets from the sun.

_____ Uranus

_____ Jupiter

_____ Pluto

_____ Neptune

_____ Saturn

**B.** Write the name of the outer planet that each sentence describes.

_____ 1. This outer planet has bands of red, yellow, brown, and white gases.

_____ 2. This outer planet has more moons than any other planet in the solar system.

_____ 3. This outer planet is the next giant after Saturn.

_____ 4. This outer planet has 8 moons.

_____ 5. This outer planet is the smallest planet in the solar system.

**C.** Write <u>True</u> if the sentence is true. Write <u>False</u> if the sentence is false.

_____ 1. All of the outer planets are giants.

_____ 2. All of the outer planets have moons.

_____ 3. All of the outer planets orbit the sun.

**D.** Write one or more sentences to answer the question.

Pluto is the coldest planet in the solar system. Why do you think this is so?

_____

_____

_____

99

## LESSON 6

# What Are Comets, Asteroids, and Meteoroids?

You have learned that the sun and the nine planets are part of the solar system. But there are many other objects in our solar system, such as **comets**, **asteroids**, and **meteoroids**.

**Comets** are icy objects that orbit the sun in long paths shaped like ovals. Astronomers sometimes call comets "dirty snowballs" because they are made mostly of frozen gases and dust. When comets move closer to the sun, energy from the sun pushes some of the comet's gases and dust out into space. The gases and dust make long tails that reflect sunlight. The comet's tail may be millions of miles long.

**Asteroids** are huge pieces of rock or metal that orbit the sun. They travel in an **asteroid belt** between Mars and Jupiter. The largest asteroid is more than six hundred miles across. Asteroids are smaller than planets, but there are many of them. Astronomers call asteroids **minor planets**.

Have you ever seen a shooting star? What you saw was really a **meteor**. A meteor is a bright streak of light in the sky. Meteors are made when small **meteoroids** enter Earth's atmosphere and burn up. Meteoroids are broken pieces of asteroids or comets. If the meteoroid is too large, it may not burn up completely. When the meteoroid falls to the ground, it is called a **meteorite**.

Meteoroids enter the Earth's atmosphere all of the time. Sometimes we see a large number of meteors coming from the same direction in the sky. As they burn, we see a **meteor shower**.

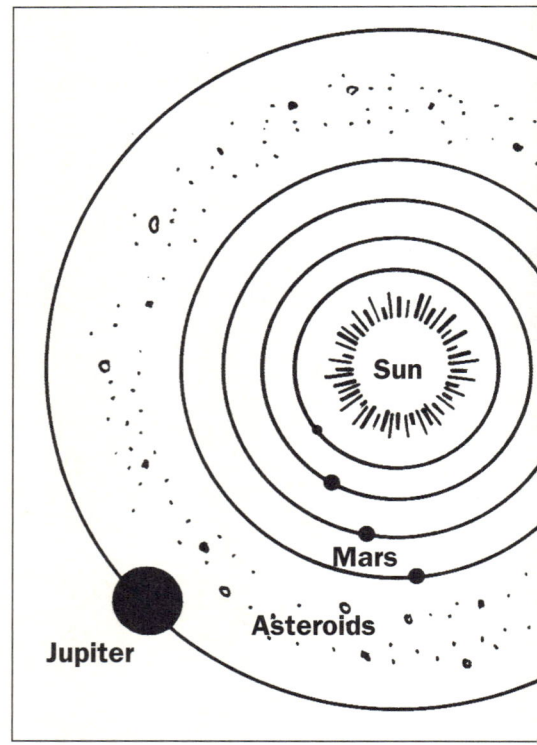

Many asteroids orbit the sun in the asteroid belt between Mars and Jupiter.

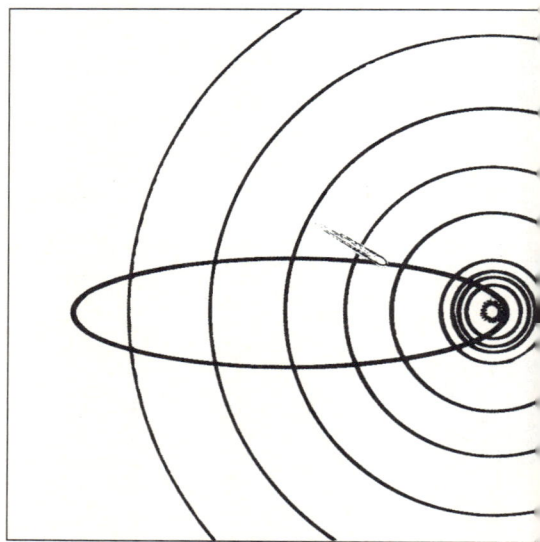

Comets orbit the sun in long paths shaped like ovals.

**A.** Draw a line between the object and the words that describe where it is found.

1. meteor             in outer space
2. meteorite          in Earth's atmosphere
3. meteoroid          on the surface of Earth

**B.** Write the word or words that best complete each sentence.

| asteroid belt | asteroids | comets | gases | ovals |

1. Comets orbit the sun in paths shaped like _____.

2. Astronomers sometimes call _____ "dirty snowballs."

3. Comets are made mostly of frozen _____ and dust.

4. Huge pieces of rock or metal that orbit the sun are called _____.

5. Most asteroids are found in the _____ between Mars and Jupiter.

**C.** Write one or more sentences to answer the question.

Asteroids are sometimes called planetoids, which means "like a planet." How are asteroids like planets?

_____
_____
_____
_____

# CHAPTER 6

# Make a Solar System Model

**You need:**

- markers
- table tennis balls
- balloons
- ruler
- tape
- construction paper
- clay

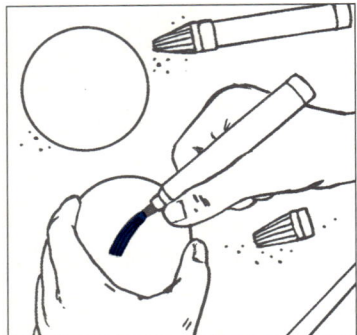

**In this activity you will make a model of our solar system.**

Follow these steps:

1. Color a table tennis ball blue. Write "Earth" on it. Color another table tennis ball light green. Write "Venus" on it.

2. Blow up an orange balloon until it is about 17 inches across. Write "Jupiter" on it. Blow up a yellow balloon until it is about 15 inches across. Write "Saturn" on it. Use construction paper to make a ring.

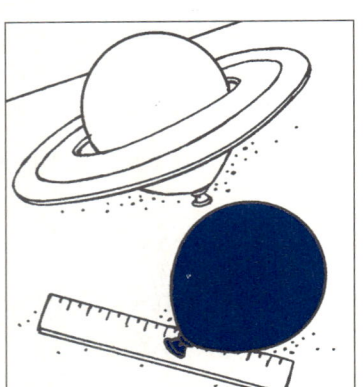

3. Blow up a light-blue balloon until it is about 6 inches across. Write "Uranus" on it. Blow up a dark-blue balloon until it is about 6 inches across. Write "Neptune" on it.

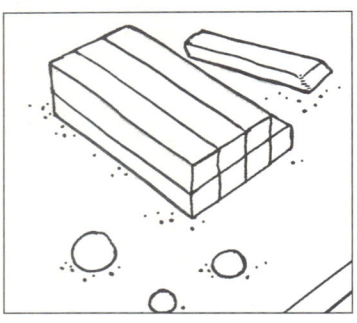

4. Make a ball of red clay $\frac{3}{4}$ inch across. Write "Ma" on it for Mars. Make a ball of blue clay $\frac{1}{3}$ inch across. Write "P" on it for Pluto. Make a ball of red clay $\frac{1}{2}$ inch across. Write "M" on it to stand for Mercury.

**Write answers to these questions.**

1. How are the inner planets like the outer planets? How are they different?

   _____

   _____

2. Which planet is about the same size as Earth?

   _____

102

# TEST CHAPTER 6

**Darken the circle next to the correct answer.**

1. Scientists who study objects in space are called
   - Ⓐ telescopes.
   - Ⓑ systems.
   - Ⓒ phases.
   - Ⓓ astronomers.

2. A tool that astronomers send into space to gather information is called
   - Ⓐ a comet.
   - Ⓑ a space probe.
   - Ⓒ a meteor.
   - Ⓓ an asteroid.

3. How many planets are there in the solar system?
   - Ⓐ three
   - Ⓑ six
   - Ⓒ nine
   - Ⓓ twelve

4. What is the force that pulls objects toward each other?
   - Ⓐ phase
   - Ⓑ gravity
   - Ⓒ rotation
   - Ⓓ orbit

5. The changes in the way the moon looks from Earth are called
   - Ⓐ craters.
   - Ⓑ crescents.
   - Ⓒ phases.
   - Ⓓ comets.

6. What is the most common landform found on the moon's surface?
   - Ⓐ asteroids
   - Ⓑ meteors
   - Ⓒ craters
   - Ⓓ comets

7. The four planets that orbit closest to the sun are called
   - Ⓐ the inner planets.
   - Ⓑ the outer planets.
   - Ⓒ moons.
   - Ⓓ giants.

8. The five planets that orbit farthest from the sun are called
   - Ⓐ the inner planets.
   - Ⓑ the outer planets.
   - Ⓒ moons.
   - Ⓓ giants.

9. Which object has a tail made of gases and dust?
   - Ⓐ a comet
   - Ⓑ a meteorite
   - Ⓒ an asteroid
   - Ⓓ a planet

10. What does a meteoroid become when it hits Earth's atmosphere?
    - Ⓐ an asteroid
    - Ⓑ a comet
    - Ⓒ a meteor
    - Ⓓ a meteorite

# Careers

## Wildlife Conservationist

Some wild animals need help from people in order to live. A wildlife conservationist plans ways to protect wild animals.

Some wildlife conservationists carry out laws that stop people from hunting and fishing for wild animals. Others help to take care of the areas where wild animals live. They make sure that wilderness areas have plenty of water and food and are clean, safe places for animals to live.

## Oceanographer

An oceanographer is a scientist who studies the ocean. Some oceanographers study animals that live in the ocean. Others study ocean water and waves or the ocean floor. They use tools to measure the movements of ocean water. They also collect information that helps people to understand the weather and to protect ocean animals.

Oceanographers sometimes work on ships and scientific study boats. Sometimes they work underwater. There they observe ocean animals.

## Astronomer

An astronomer studies the stars and planets, the moon, comets, and asteroids. Thousands of years ago, astronomers learned about the movements of stars and planets by watching the stars with just their eyes. Today, astronomers use telescopes and computers. They also use information that astronauts collect on trips into outer space.

# Unit 3
# Physical Science

You are standing on a corner when you hear shrill sounds and see flashing lights. People stop and look around. You still can hear the sounds and see the lights. Suddenly, the fire engine roars around a corner and drives past. How did the sounds and the lights reach you? In this chapter you will learn about the special nature of light and sound.

# CHAPTER 7

# Energy

It may not look like it, but light is made of many different colors. Special objects called prisms bend light and divide the colors into bands. Raindrops can do the same thing. So, when light shines through raindrops, you may see a rainbow. In this chapter you will learn more about light.

## What is it?

- It can push or pull objects.
- It can pick up pieces of metal.
- It has a north pole and a south pole.

# LESSON 1

# What Is Light?

Imagine a world that had no colors. It wouldn't be as beautiful as the world we see every day. And colors are important to living things. Colors help an animal hide. Colors can also help animals find food. For example, butterflies and many other insects get food from flowers. They find flowers using color.

We see colors because light has colors in it. Bright light, like light from the sun or from a bright lightbulb, is called **white light**. White light is made of red, green, blue, and other colors mixed together. It is light that gives every object its color.

When you turn on a lightbulb, the light from the bulb travels out and hits each object in the room. Each object takes in part of the light, and bounces some light back to your eyes. We see only the part of light that bounces back. So if a chair looks red to us, it is because the chair bounces back the red part of light. For the same reason, if the chair looks green, it is because the chair bounces back the green part of light.

You can see the colors that are in white light by shining light through a special piece of glass called a **prism**. As the light moves through the prism, it bends. When the light bends, the colors in the light spread out.

A rain shower can be like a giant prism in the sky. When sunlight goes through the raindrops, it bends. The colors in the sunlight spread apart. You see the colors that make up sunlight as a rainbow.

**Light Passing Through a Prism**

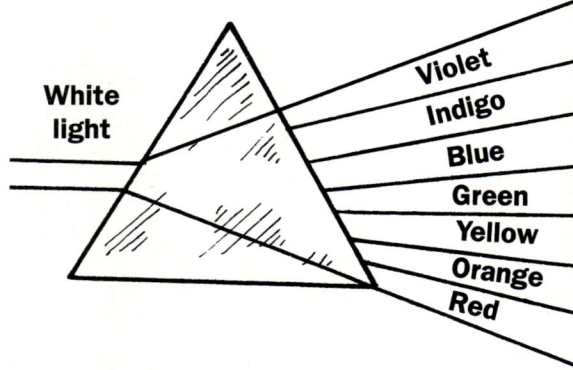

A prism splits apart the different colors that blend together to make white light.

**A.** **Draw a line to complete each sentence.**

1. White light       is made when raindrops act like a giant prism.

2. A prism           can come from the sun or from a lightbulb.

3. A rainbow         is a special piece of glass that spreads the colors of light.

**B.** **Write the missing word or words in each sentence.**

1. Many insects find flowers using _____.

   (prisms, raindrops, color)

2. White light is made of _____.

   (the color white, many colors mixed together, three colors mixed together)

3. A blue chair bounces back the _____ part of light.

   (white, blue, yellow)

4. A prism _____ light to spread it apart.

   (bends, stops, bounces back)

5. The colors of a rainbow are the colors that make up _____.

   (air, sunlight, water)

**C.** **Write one or more sentences to answer the questions.**

Imagine you are in a room lit by a special lightbulb. The white light from this bulb is made up of all the colors except red. Would you be able to see the color red in this room? Why or why not?

_____
_____
_____
_____

# LESSON 2
## How Does Light Travel?

Light is a kind of energy. Light travels in a straight line until it strikes an object. When it strikes an object, light can be **reflected**, **absorbed**, or **refracted**.

You have learned that you could see a red chair if the chair bounced the red part of light back to your eyes. When light bounces back from an object, it is called **reflected** light. Light can be reflected in different amounts. How much light an object reflects depends on how smooth the object is and what color it is. Smooth objects, like mirrors, reflect light very well. White or other bright objects also reflect light well.

Rough objects or ones that are black or dark do not reflect light as well. These objects have taken in, or a**bsorbed**, more light than they have bounced back. If you were in a dark cave and pointed the beam of your flashlight at a wall of dark, rough rocks, you would still find it difficult to see. The rocks in the cave would have absorbed much of the light from your flashlight. If the cave walls were made of light, smooth rocks, they would not absorb as much light, and you would find it easier to see.

Some objects allow light to pass through. For example, light passes easily through water and glass. But when light passes through water or glass, it slows down. When it slows down, light bends. When light bends, we say it is **refracted**. You can see how light refracts if you put a pencil in a glass of water. Look at the part of the pencil that is under water. It will look bent.

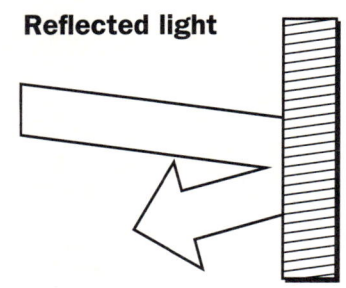

**Reflected light**

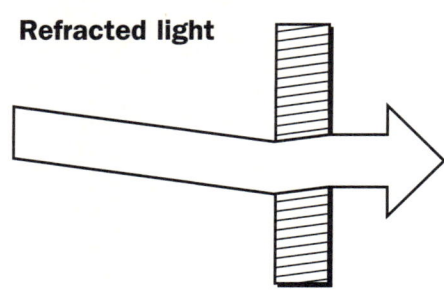

**Refracted light**

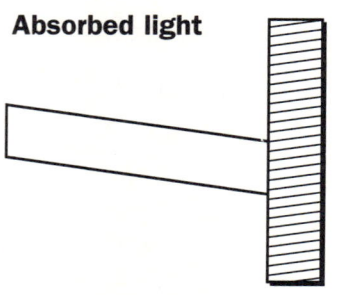

**Absorbed light**

When light hits an object, it can be reflected, refracted, or absorbed.

## A. Write the word that best completes each sentence.

absorbed    reflected    refracted

1. Light that bounces back from objects is called _____ light.

2. When an object takes light in, the light is _____.

3. Light that passes through an object and bends is _____.

## B. Write True if the sentence is true. Write False if the sentence is false.

_____ 1. Light is a kind of energy.

_____ 2. Light usually travels in circles.

_____ 3. Smooth, white objects reflect light well.

_____ 4. Dark, rough objects absorb light.

_____ 5. Light doesn't pass through glass.

_____ 6. When light passes through water, the light is refracted.

## C. Write one or more sentences to answer the questions.

Pretend there is a hole in the road. Your job is to make a marker to keep cars away from the hole. The marker needs to be easy to see at night, when cars shine their headlights on it. You can make a smooth, bright yellow marker, or a rough, dark blue one. Which one would be better? Why?

_____
_____
_____
_____
_____

LESSON

# 3  What Is Sound?

Think of all the different sounds you've heard today. Did you hear the alarm on your clock this morning? Did you hear a dog bark or a bird sing? Maybe you heard a car's horn. Maybe you heard music on the radio.

All these sounds are very different, but they have one thing in common. When an object **vibrates**, or moves back and forth very fast, it makes sound. Place your fingers gently against the middle of your throat. Now, say a word. You should be able to feel the vibration from the sound of your voice.

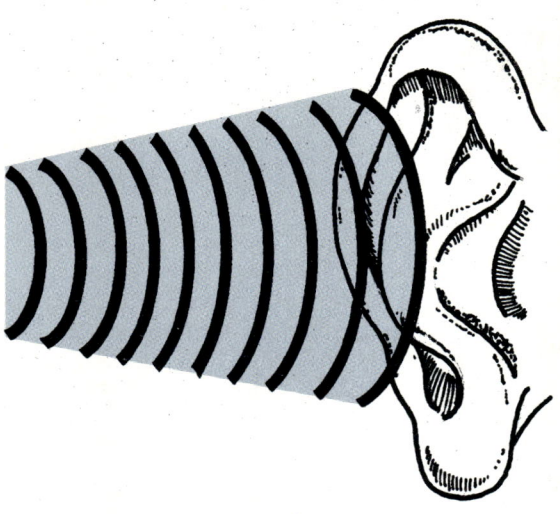

Sound travels in a sound wave.

Vibration causes sound to travel through air, water, and even through metal or rock. Most of the sounds that we hear travel through air.

Imagine a woman playing a drum. When she hits the drum, the top of the drum vibrates. It pushes the air next to it back and forth. This squeezes the air, then stretches it out, over and over again. All this squeezing and stretching makes the air bump into other air that is a little farther away. The back and forth motion gets passed along through the air in a **sound wave**. When a sound wave reaches your ear, you hear the sound.

Some vibrations are faster than others. How fast an object vibrates makes it sound high or low. The highness or lowness of a sound is called its **pitch**. Faster vibrations make higher sounds. Sounds made by vibrations can also be loud or soft. The loudness or softness of a sound is called its **volume**.

## A.

**Underline the correct word or words in each sentence.**

1. All sounds are made by (metal, air, vibrations).

2. Sounds can travel (through different things, only in water, only through air).

3. Sound travels through the air in a (straight line, curved path, sound wave).

4. The highness or lowness of a sound is its (volume, pitch, wave).

5. The loudness or softness of a sound is its (vibration, volume, pitch).

## B.

**Below is a list of things that happen when we hear the sound of a drum. Write 1, 2, 3, 4, and 5 to show the correct order. The first one is done for you.**

_____ The back and forth movement is passed along in a sound wave.

_____ The top of the drum vibrates.

___1___ A woman hits a drum.

_____ The sound wave reaches your ear and you hear the sound.

_____ The top of the drum pushes the air next to it back and forth.

## C.

**Write one or more sentences to answer the questions.**

When a tiny bird sings, its throat vibrates very fast. When an owl hoots, its throat vibrates more slowly than the tiny bird's does. When you hear these sounds, which one sounds higher? Why?

_____
_____
_____
_____
_____
_____

# LESSON 4

## What Is a Magnet?

A **magnet** is a special object that pulls or pushes other magnets or pieces of metal. It does this because of a force you cannot see. This force is called **magnetism**.

Because of magnetism, magnets can push or pull on objects without even touching them. Sometimes you can pick objects up with a magnet. Some magnets might pick up a piece of metal the size of a paper clip. Others are strong enough to pick up a car.

Magnets always have two ends, called **poles**. The magnetism in the magnet is strongest at the poles. One of the poles is called **north**, and the other is called **south**.

The poles of a magnet make it act a certain way. Imagine that you put two straight magnets on a table, with the ends of the magnets almost touching. As soon as you put them down, the ends of the magnets pull toward each other and stick together. Then you flip one of the magnets over and put it down again. Now the magnets want to push away from each other. Why?

We know that each magnet has a pole at each end. If you put the north pole of one magnet next to the south pole of another magnet, the two magnets pull toward each other. But if you put the two north poles together, they push away from each other. This happens with two south poles, too. Poles that are the same always push away from each other. If poles are different, they pull toward each other.

**The Poles of a Magnet**

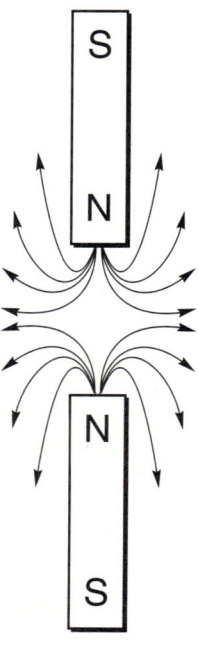

Poles that are the same push away from each other.

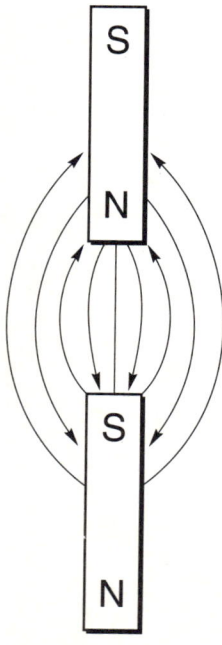

Poles that are different pull toward each other.

**A.** Write **True** if the sentence is true. Write **False** if the sentence is false.

_____ 1. Magnets can push or pull other magnets and metal.

_____ 2. Magnets can only pick up very small pieces of metal.

_____ 3. The ends of a magnet are called its poles.

_____ 4. A magnet's poles are called north and south.

_____ 5. Magnets never try to push away from each other.

**B.** Below are drawings of magnets next to each other. Underline the correct word or words in the sentence under each drawing.

```
[ S     N ]          [ S     N ]

[ N     S ]          [ S     N ]
```

1. These two magnets will (pull toward, push away from) each other.

2. These two magnets will (pull toward, push away from) each other.

**C.** Write one or more sentences to answer the question.

Imagine that you are making a small box to keep objects in. You put a door on the box, but it won't stay closed. You decide to use two magnets to help hold it closed. You plan to glue one magnet to the edge of the box, and the other to the inside of the door, where it will touch the first one. How should you put the magnets so they will keep the door and the edge of the box together?

_____

_____

_____

# LESSON 5

## How Is Electricity Used?

Imagine how different life would be without lights, televisions, refrigerators, and telephones. What if we didn't have any of these things? We have all these things, and many more, because of **electricity**. Electricity makes them work. Electricity is a very important kind of energy.

People use electricity all the time. Life would be more difficult without electricity. Even if we lit candles to see, it would be much darker at night. It would be hard to cook food, or to keep the food cold so it didn't spoil. Washing clothes would be very tiring. There would be no radio to listen to or television to watch.

One of the main ways that people use electricity is to make light. Electricity makes the inside of a bulb shine brightly. Think of all the different kinds of lights that help people. Lights inside your home let you see at night. Streetlights and traffic lights make roads safer for cars. Headlights, flashlights, and work lights all help make life easier.

Electricity helps people by making heat. People use heat from electricity to keep their homes warm and to cook food. Heat from electricity is also used to help build things like bicycles and ships.

People also use electricity to make sound. Electricity makes sound by making objects vibrate. The ringing of a telephone, the music on the radio, and the buzz of an alarm clock all are sounds made by electricity.

**Ways That People Use Electricity**

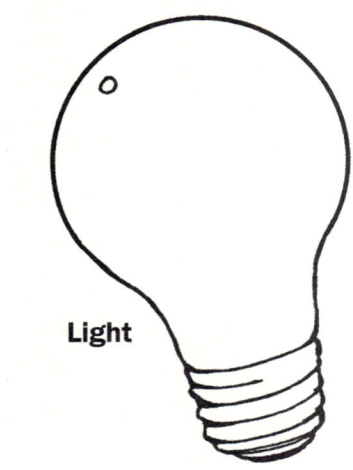
Light

Heat

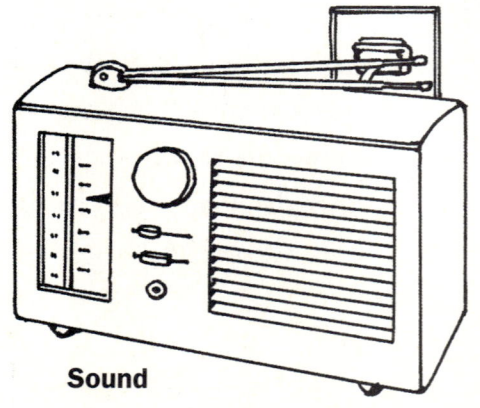
Sound

## A. Write the missing word or words in each sentence.

1. Electricity is a kind of _____.
   (light, heat, energy)

2. Life would be _____ without electricity.
   (more difficult, easier, longer)

3. People use electricity to make light, heat, and _____.
   (radios, lightbulbs, sound)

## B. Write a sentence about each of the following ways we use electricity.

1. the way we use light

   _____
   _____

2. the way we use heat

   _____
   _____

3. the way we use sound

   _____
   _____

## C. Write one or more sentences to answer the questions.

A hundred years ago, most people didn't have electricity in their homes. They had to wash clothes, cook food, and warm their homes without electricity. Would these jobs have been easier or more difficult a hundred years ago? How does electricity help us do these jobs now?

_____
_____
_____
_____

# LESSON 6

## What Is a Circuit?

Electricity always travels in a circle. The circle that electricity travels in is called a **circuit**. Electrical circuits can be different sizes. Circuits that are inside something like a radio might be so small that they are hard to see. But electrical circuits that are carried by power lines can cover miles and miles.

The electrical circuit inside a flashlight makes it work. Flashlights have one or more **batteries**. The batteries are where the electricity starts. They push the electricity around the circle. Inside one end of the flashlight is a small lightbulb. Wires run from the batteries to the bulb. The electricity goes from the batteries, through one wire, through the bulb, through the other wire, and back to the battery. When the electricity passes through the bulb, it lights up.

Another kind of electrical circuit is the one that brings electricity to your home. This is a much bigger circuit than the one in the flashlight! But it works the same way.

The electricity in your home comes from a place that makes electricity, called a **power plant**. Long wires reach from the power plant to your home, then back again. The wires may be held up on poles or buried underground. If the power plant is far away, these wires might be miles and miles in length. The wires make a big circle. The power plant pushes electricity through the wires, to your home and back again. If there were no circuits, electricity wouldn't be able to flow.

**An Electrical Circuit**

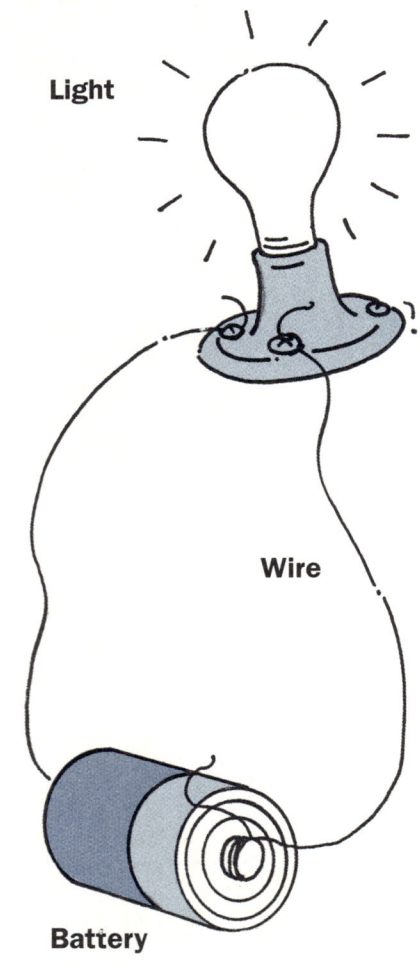

Light

Wire

Battery

**A.** Write the word or words that best complete each sentence.

| battery | circuit | power plant | travels |

1. Electricity always _____ in a circle.

2. The circle that electricity travels in is called a _____.

3. Inside a flashlight, electricity comes from the _____.

4. Electricity travels on wires from a _____ to your home.

**B.** Look at the diagram shown here. In this diagram, the electricity cannot travel. Change the diagram so electricity will be able to travel.

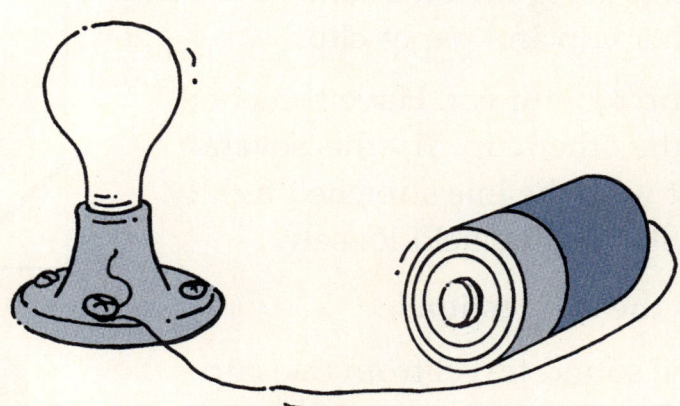

**C.** Write one or more sentences to answer the questions.

Wires carry electricity between a power plant and your home. If an ice storm makes these wires break apart, will you be able to turn on the lights or cook on the stove in your home? Why or why not?

_____

_____

# CHAPTER 7

# Make a Telephone

**You need:**

- dental floss or fishing line
- 3 paper clips
- 2 paper cups

**In this activity you will make a simple telephone.**

Follow these steps:

1. Cut a piece of line about 15 feet long. Then, bend a paper clip like the one in the picture.

2. Use the bent paper clip to poke a small hole in the bottom of one cup. Put one end of the line through the hole. Tie that end to a paper clip inside the cup.

3. Repeat Step 2, using the other end of the line with the other cup and paper clip.

4. Hold one cup to your ear. Have someone speak into the other cup. Try this several times. Try it with the line stretched tightly. Then, try with the line held loosely.

**Write answers to these questions.**

1. How did the sound travel from one cup to the other?

   _____

   _____

2. How did the sound change when you held the line tightly or loosely? Why do you think this was so?

   _____

   _____

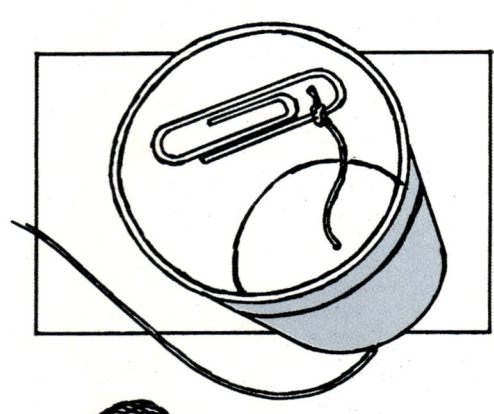

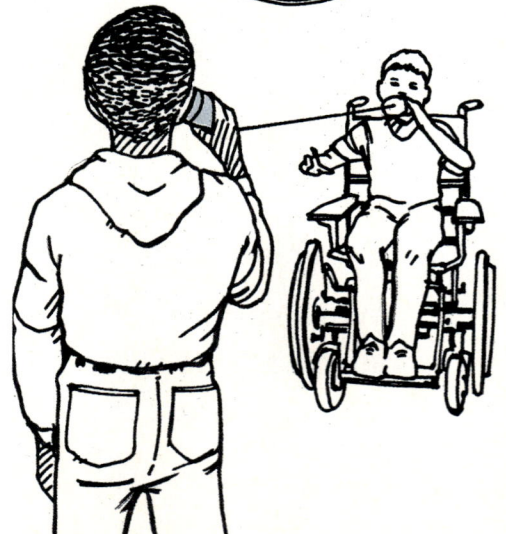

# TEST CHAPTER 7

**Darken the circle next to the correct answer.**

1. Bright light from the sun or from a lightbulb is called
   - Ⓐ colored light.
   - Ⓑ white light.
   - Ⓒ blended light.
   - Ⓓ rainbow light.

2. A piece of glass that bends light to spread it into colors is a
   - Ⓐ tube.
   - Ⓑ vase.
   - Ⓒ prism.
   - Ⓓ bulb.

3. What is light that bounces off of objects called?
   - Ⓐ reflected light
   - Ⓑ bounced light
   - Ⓒ absorbed light
   - Ⓓ refracted light

4. When light passes through an object and is bent, it is called
   - Ⓐ reflected light.
   - Ⓑ bounced light.
   - Ⓒ absorbed light.
   - Ⓓ refracted light.

5. Sound travels through air and other things in a
   - Ⓐ sound line.
   - Ⓑ pitch.
   - Ⓒ sound wave.
   - Ⓓ volume.

6. What is the highness or lowness of sound called?
   - Ⓐ refraction
   - Ⓑ wave
   - Ⓒ volume
   - Ⓓ pitch

7. When the north poles of two magnets are put together, they
   - Ⓐ pull together.
   - Ⓑ push apart.
   - Ⓒ pull up.
   - Ⓓ do nothing.

8. Electricity can make sound by making objects
   - Ⓐ vibrate.
   - Ⓑ heat up.
   - Ⓒ light up.
   - Ⓓ move in a circle.

9. The circle that electricity travels in is called a
   - Ⓐ prism.
   - Ⓑ vibration.
   - Ⓒ sound wave.
   - Ⓓ circuit.

10. Electricity travels through long wires to your home from a
    - Ⓐ flashlight.
    - Ⓑ power plant.
    - Ⓒ battery.
    - Ⓓ lightbulb.

# Careers

## Photographer

A photographer takes pictures. Some photographers take pictures for books, magazines, and newspapers. Others film television shows and movies. Some photographers travel all over the world. Some may even work underwater!

A photographer's main tool is a camera, but photographers also use machines to develop film. Many photographers use computers to make changes to their photographs.

## Optical Engineer

An optical engineer designs tools that use light. Cameras use light. An optical engineer designs cameras that take photographs. They also design the cameras that make the movies you watch at the theater. Telescopes and computers also use light.

You may have seen a special photograph called a hologram on a magazine cover, a credit card, or in a museum. Engineers who make holograms use laser light, lenses, and mirrors. Holograms make objects look deeper than objects in regular photographs. This special kind of photography is called holography. Scientists use holography to make maps, study machine parts, and store computer information.

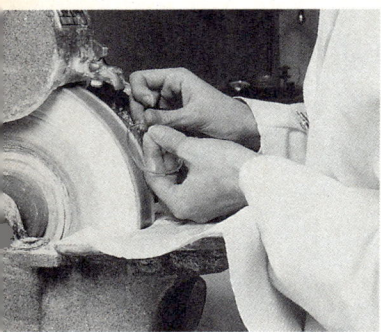

## Lens Grinder

A lens grinder sets up and runs the machines that make lenses for eyeglasses, telescopes, cameras, and other goods. If you wear eyeglasses, then you know that lenses can help you to see better. Astronomers use lenses, too, in their telescopes.

Lenses are pieces of glass with round surfaces. Lens grinders may polish the pieces of glass for many hours to make their surfaces smooth.

# Glossary

**A**    **absorbed light**, page 110.
Absorbed light is not reflected by an object but is taken in by the object.

**abyss**, page 82.
The abyss is the deepest part of the ocean.

**asteroid belt**, page 100.
A large number of asteroids travels in an asteroid belt between Mars and Jupiter.

**asteroids**, page 100.
Asteroids are huge pieces of rock or metal that orbit the sun.

**astronauts**, page 94.
Astronauts are people who are specially trained to travel into and study space.

**astronomers**, page 90.
Astronomers are scientists who study stars and other objects in space.

**atmosphere**, page 96.
An atmosphere is a layer of air that surrounds a planet.

**B**    **batteries**, page 118.
A battery can be used as part of an electric circuit.

**C**    **carbon dioxide**, page 12.
Carbon dioxide is a gas in the air. Plants use it to make food. Animals breathe it out as a waste.

**carnivores**, page 60.
Carnivores are animals that eat only other animals.

**cells**, page 10.
The cell is the smallest living part of all living things.

**characteristics**, page 34.
Characteristics are qualities. Two characteristics of crickets are that they have six legs and an exoskeleton.

**chlorophyll**, page 12.
Chlorophyll is a chemical in green plants. It traps the sun's energy so plants can make food.

**circuit**, page 118.
A circuit is a circle in which electricity travels.

**cochlea**, page 44.
The cochlea is part of the inner ear. It is filled with fluid and contains receptor cells. It changes sound into signals to the brain.

**cold-blooded**, page 26.
A cold-blooded animal's body temperature changes with the outside temperature.

**comets**, page 100.
Comets are icy objects that orbit the sun in long paths shaped like ovals.

**compete**, page 62.
In some games you compete, or try to win. Each living thing competes to win what it needs to live.

**competition**, page 62.
Competing with other living things is called competition.

**cones**, page 42.
Cones are one of the two kinds of receptor cells in the retina. Cones sense bright light and colors.

**conifers**, page 18.
Conifers are plants that have seed cones instead of flowers.

**consumers**, page 60.
Consumers are living things that use other living things for food.

**continental shelf**, page 82.
The continental shelf is the part of the ocean floor closest to land.

**craters**, page 94.
Craters, the most common landforms on the moon, are holes in the ground.

**crescent moon**, page 94.
A crescent moon is thin and looks like an eyelash.

**crust**, page 78.
The crust is the outside layer of Earth. It is made of rocks.

D **day**, page 92.
A day is the time it takes Earth to rotate once on its axis.

**decomposers**, page 60.
Decomposers are tiny living things that get their energy by eating dead plants and animals.

**digest**, page 28.
An animal's body must digest, or break down, the food the animal eats.

E **eardrum**, page 44.
The eardrum is a piece of tissue that is pulled tight like the top of a drum. It is the last part of the outer ear.

**Earth**, page 96.
Earth is the third planet from the sun.

**earthquake**, page 78.
In an earthquake, Earth shakes because plates in its crust push, pull, or rub each other with great force.

**ecosystem**, page 58.
An ecosystem is a community of plants and animals in an area.

**eggs**, page 18.
The female parts of flowers make eggs.

**electricity**, page 116.
Electricity is an important kind of energy that is used to make light and heat.

**erosion**, page 76.
Erosion is the carrying away of broken pieces of landforms by wind and water.

**erupt**, page 78.
Volcanoes can erupt, or explode, and shoot out melted rock.

**exoskeleton**, page 26.
An exoskeleton is an outside skeleton, like a grasshopper's hard shell.

**extinct**, page 64.
An animal or a plant is extinct when none of its kind are left on Earth.

F **flowering plants**, page 18.
Flowering plants grow flowers to make seeds from which new plants grow.

**food chain**, page 60.
A food chain is how food energy moves through an ecosystem. For example, grass is eaten by a cricket, the cricket is eaten by a frog, and the frog is eaten by a hawk.

**full moon**, page 94.
A full moon looks round.

G **gravity**, page 92.
Gravity is the force that pulls objects toward each other.

H **hearing**, page 40.
Hearing is the sense that uses the ears to pick up sounds.

**herbivores**, page 60.
Herbivores are living things that eat only plants.

**hill**, page 74.
A hill rises above the land around it, but not as high as a mountain does.

I **igneous rock**, page 80.
Igneous rock is rock that forms when melted rock from inside Earth cools.

**inherit**, page 34.
You inherit a characteristic if it is passed to you from your parents.

**inner ear**, page 44.
The inner ear contains the cochlea, which changes sound into nerve signals that go to the brain.

**inner planets**, page 96.
The inner planets orbit closest to the sun. They are Mercury, Venus, Earth, and Mars.

**intestines**, page 28.
Intestines are organs that help an animal digest food. Blood carries digested food to the rest of the body.

**invertebrates**, page 26.
Invertebrates like crickets do not have a backbone.

**iris**, page 42.
The iris is the colored part of the eye.

J **Jupiter**, page 98.
Jupiter, the fifth planet from the sun, is the largest planet in the solar system.

L **landform**, page 74.
A landform is a shape on Earth's surface.

**landslide**, page 78.
A landslide is when loose rocks and soil tumble down steep mountains.

**layers**, page 78.
Earth is made of layers. Each layer is like a separate cover or blanket.

**leaves**, page 8.
Leaves are parts of plants. They make most of the plant's food.

**lens**, page 42.
The lens of the eye is behind the pupil. It bends light that enters the eye.

**life cycle**, page 18.
A life cycle is how a living thing grows and changes.

M **magnet**, page 114.
A magnet is an object that pushes or pulls other magnets or pieces of metal.

**magnetism**, page 114.
Magnetism is the force that a magnet has.

**mammals**, page 32.
Mammals are animals that have hair and feed their young with milk.

**Mars**, page 96.
Mars is the fourth planet from the sun.

**Mercury**, page 96.
Mercury, the planet closest to the sun, is the smallest of the inner planets.

**metamorphic rock**, page 80.
Metamorphic rock forms deep inside Earth when heat and squeezing change other rocks.

**meteor**, page 100.
A meteor is a streak of light in the sky made when a small meteoroid enters Earth's atmosphere and burns up.

**meteorite**, page 100.
A meteorite is a meteoroid that falls to the ground.

**meteoroids**, page 100.
Meteoroids are broken pieces of asteroids or comets.

**meteor shower**, page 100.
A meteor shower is a large number of meteors coming from the same direction and burning in the sky.

**microscope**, page 10.
A microscope is a tool that makes objects like plant cells look larger.

**middle ear**, page 44.
The middle ear contains three tiny bones that pass sound from the outer ear to the inner ear.

**minor planets**, page 100.
Minor planets is another name for asteroids.

**moon**, page 94.
The moon is Earth's partner in space. It orbits Earth about once each month.

**mountain**, page 74.
A mountain is the highest landform, or shape, on Earth's surface.

N **nature preserves**, page 68.
Nature preserves are special parks where plants and animals live and the ecosystems are protected.

**Neptune**, page 98.
Neptune is the giant planet that is farthest from the sun.

**nerve cells**, page 40.
Nerve cells form pathways for messages to and from your brain.

**nervous system**, page 40.
Your nervous system includes the pathways of nerve cells in your body and your brain.

**nonliving things**, page 58.
Nonliving things are things like rocks, water, air, and soil.

**north pole**, page 114.
The north pole is one end of a magnet.

**nutrients**, page 14.
Nutrients are special matter that plants need to grow and stay healthy. They enter a plant through the roots.

**O** **ocean currents**, page 82.
Ocean currents are rivers of water that flow through the ocean around them.

**ocean floor**, page 82.
The bottom of the ocean is the ocean floor.

**odors**, page 46.
Odors are smells in the air.

**oil**, page 84.
People use oil to run factories and cars and to heat homes. Large machines dig deep under the sea to find oil.

**oil spill**, page 84.
An oil spill happens when an oil tanker crashes or sinks and oil leaks out into the ocean.

**olfactory cells**, page 46.
Olfactory cells are receptor cells in the nose that sense odors and send signals to the brain.

**omnivores**, page 60.
Omnivores are consumers that eat both plants and animals.

**open ocean**, page 82.
The open ocean is the part of the ocean far away from the shore.

**optical telescope**, page 90.
An optical telescope is a tool that collects light waves. It makes objects that are far away look closer.

**optic nerve**, page 42.
The optic nerve carries signals to the brain from the rods and cones in the retina.

**orbit**, page 92.
To orbit means to circle, or go around.

**organization**, page 10.
Living things show organization because smaller parts make up larger parts.

**organs**, page 24.
Organs, such as the stomach, are animal parts made of different kinds of tissues that work together.

**outer ear**, page 44.
The outer ear is the part of the ear you can see. It guides sound toward the eardrum.

**outer planets**, page 98.
The outer planets are the five planets farthest from the sun. They are Jupiter, Saturn, Uranus, Neptune, and Pluto.

**oxygen**, page 12.
Oxygen is a gas that comes from the air. Plants give it off as a waste. Animals need it to live.

**P** **phases of the moon**, page 94.
The phases of the moon are the changes in the way the moon looks from Earth.

**phloem**, page 14.
Phloem are tubes found in plants. They move food around the plant.

**photosynthesis**, page 12.
Photosynthesis is the process that plants use to make food.

**pitch**, page 112.
The pitch of a sound is how high or low it is.

**plain**, page 74.
A plain is the lowest type of landform. It is mostly flat or gently rolling.

**planets**, page 92.
Planets are the largest objects that orbit the sun. There are nine planets.

**plateau**, page 74.
A plateau is a landform that can rise as high as a mountain, but is flat on top.

**plates**, page 78.
Earth's crust is made of large pieces called plates.

**Pluto**, page 98.
Pluto is the last known planet in the solar system. It is the smallest planet.

**poles**, page 114.
The poles are the ends of a magnet.

**pollen**, page 18.
The male parts of flowers make tiny grains called pollen.

**pollution**, page 66.
Pollution is harmful waste that is put in the air, land, or water.

**power plant**, page 118.
A power plant is one place where electricity starts.

**prescription drugs**, page 50.
Prescription drugs are medicines that a doctor orders for you from a drugstore.

**pressure receptor cells**, page 48.
Pressure receptor cells sense when something is touching your skin.

**prism**, page 108.
A prism is a special piece of glass that splits white light into its many colors.

**process**, page 12.
A process is a group of steps that must take place in a specific order for something to happen.

**producers**, page 60.
Producers are living things that make food.

**pupil**, page 42.
The pupil is the black circle in the center of the eye.

**R** **radio telescope**, page 90.
A radio telescope collects radio waves. Astronomers use computers to study these waves and learn about space.

**receptor cells**, page 40.
Receptor cells are special cells that help you to sense things, like sounds, colors, smells, and tastes.

**recycle**, page 68.
To recycle waste means to use old things to make new things.

**reduce**, page 68.
To reduce waste means to use fewer things that can cause pollution.

**reflected light**, page 110.
Reflected light is light that bounces back from an object.

**refracted light**, page 110.
Refracted light is light that is bent when it passes through an object.

**reproduce**, page 18.
When a living thing reproduces, it makes new living things like itself.

**retina**, page 42.
The retina is a layer of tissue inside the eye, at the back of the eyeball.

**reuse**, page 68.
To reuse means to use things over again instead of throwing them away.

**rods**, page 42.
Rods are one of the two kinds of receptor cells in the retina. Rods sense dim light.

**roots**, page 8.
Roots are parts of plants. They take in water and other materials from the soil. They also hold the plant in the soil.

**rotate**, page 92.
To rotate means to spin like a top.

**S** **Saturn**, page 98.
Saturn is the sixth planet from the sun. It has large rings made of ice.

**sedimentary rock**, page 80.
Sedimentary rock forms when small pieces of other rocks or parts of dead plants or animals are pressed together very hard.

**sense organs**, page 40.
Your sense organs are your eyes, ears, tongue, nose, and skin.

**ships**, page 84.
Ships travel on the ocean, bringing food, clothing, and other things to different parts of the world.

**sight**, page 40.
Sight is using the eyes to see.

**skeleton**, page 24.
An animal's skeleton is a frame made of bones. It holds up the animal's body.

**skin**, page 24.
The skin is the organ that protects an animal's body.

**smell**, page 40.
Smell is the sense that uses the nose to pick up odors.

**solar system**, page 92.
The solar system is the sun and everything that circles it.

**sound wave**, page 112.
A sound wave is produced when a vibrating object makes the air vibrate.

**south pole**, page 114.
The south pole is one end of a magnet.

**space probe**, page 90.
A space probe is a spacecraft sent into space to explore.

**stems**, page 8.
Stems are parts of plants. They hold the plant up. They also carry water and food through the plant.

**stomach**, page 28.
The stomach is an organ that helps an animal digest its food.

**stomata**, page 12.
Stomata are small openings in plant leaves.

**T** **tankers**, page 84.
Tankers are huge ships that carry oil.

**taste**, page 40.
Taste is the sense that uses the tongue to pick up flavors.

**taste buds**, page 46.
Taste buds are the receptor cells for taste. They are on your tongue.

**tissues**, page 10.
Tissues are groups of the same kind of cells working together.

**touch**, page 40.
Touch is the sense that uses the nerves to pick up feelings like heat and pain.

**U** **Uranus**, page 98.
Uranus is the seventh planet from the sun.

**V** **Venus**, page 96.
Venus is the second planet from the sun. It is Earth's closest neighbor of the planets.

**vertebrates**, page 26.
Vertebrates are animals, like fish, whales, and humans, that have a backbone.

**vibrates**, page 112.
An object vibrates when it moves back and forth very fast.

**volcano**, page 78.
A volcano is a crack in Earth's crust where hot, melted rock spills out.

**volume**, page 112.
The volume of a sound is how loud or soft it is.

**W** **warm-blooded**, page 26.
A warm-blooded animal's body temperature always stays about the same, even if the outside temperature changes.

**weathering**, page 76.
Weathering is the breaking and wearing away of landforms.

**white light**, page 108.
White light is bright light, like light from the sun or from a bright lightbulb.

**X** **xylem**, page 14.
Xylem are tubes found in plants. They move water and nutrients from the roots to the stems and leaves.

**Y** **year**, page 92.
A year is the time Earth takes to make one complete circle around the sun.